E D

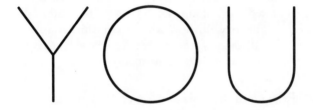

WHEN

TRUST, SURRENDER, AND THE

YOU

TRANSFORMATION OF YOUR SOUL

PRAY

ASCENSION
West Chester, Pennsylvania

Ascension
PO Box 1990
West Chester, PA 19380
1-800-376-0520
ascensionpress.com

Cover design: Faceout Studio

Printed in United States of America
23 24 25 26 27 5 4 3 2 1

ISBN 978-1-954881-94-5

To Father Paul Murray, OP

Contents

Introduction:
The Interior Pilgrimage of Prayer

Right here, at the beginning of this book, it's important to grasp this important spiritual point: *There is a great difference between a pilgrim and a tourist.*

A pilgrim and a tourist can walk into the same church in Rome or the Holy Land and have two vastly different experiences. A tourist might admire the beauty, learn the history, and even appreciate something about the spiritual significance the place holds for Christians.

A pilgrim, however, enters the same sacred space for one essential purpose: to encounter the Lord Jesus.

A true Christian pilgrim does not run into the church merely to see something—to take a photo, accomplish an item on the bucket list, or feel good about being able to tell others, "I was there!" A pilgrim does not aim just to learn some facts. Nor does the pilgrim merely enjoy the beauty of the sacred place—and then run off to be awed by the next magnificent site on the itinerary.

The pilgrim, rather, takes time to spiritually enter into the sacred place—or even better, he allows the sacredness of the site to enter him. The significance of what happened at this very spot, the example of the saint buried here, the Christian truth being celebrated in the stone, art, and glass—all are meant to become a part of us and move our hearts. A true pilgrim hopes to experience an encounter with the living God, who wants to touch our lives and lead us to take the next step in our walk with him.

The same is true in the pilgrimage of prayer. Jesus wants to take us on an interior journey with him through our prayer life. He doesn't just want us to *say* our prayers and complete a good

Christian task each day to check off a box. He doesn't just want us to learn some important facts about him in prayer. Prayer is not primarily about reading, learning, or using a certain method correctly. It's not just about the head. God ultimately wants to reach our hearts. He wants to get under the surface of our routine life and touch the deep caverns of our soul.

This is not a book about the concept of prayer or ways to pray. *It's more about learning how to cooperate with God during prayer and allowing him to act more fully in our lives.* Through our prayer, God wants to help us to grow in greater trust and surrender. He wants to liberate us from all the fear and anxiety that come from the temptation to control everything. He wants to root out the many sins, attachments, weaknesses, and disordered desires that weigh us down and keep us from giving ourselves fully to him.

Most of all, he wants to help us grow in faith, hope, and charity so that we can know, love, and worship God with all our heart, soul, strength, and mind. Indeed, Christ calls us to be made perfect in him, conformed to his very image (Romans 8:26) and changed "into his likeness, from one degree of glory to another" (2 Corinthians 3:18).

But some of us might wonder, "Is this transformation really possible for someone like me? I have many problems, struggles, and shortcomings. I'm just an ordinary Christian, not a spectacular canonized saint. Can I really come to experience Christ changing me and perfecting *me*?"

The answer is unequivocally yes! But this can happen only if we are willing to go deeper with God into the interior life of prayer.

The Interior Journey

This book aims to help guide you on the journey of prayer and bring you into the heart of Catholic spirituality. But it is very different from most other Catholic books, which are about the Scriptures, the Mass, Mary, or other aspects of the Catholic Faith.

This book goes much deeper into our interior lives. It is not just a book *about* the Catholic Faith or a book *about* prayer; it's a book that ideally should be used *in* prayer.

This book contains thirty short reflections on important themes in Catholic spirituality. I invite you to take one reflection at a time, reading it slowly and prayerfully, preferably during your own prayer time, whether at home or in the chapel. This is not a book to be read quickly. Just as a Christian does not want to enter a church with a "drive-by pilgrimage" approach—run in, take a photo, and run out—you don't want to read this book quickly from cover to cover hoping merely to come away with a few insights about the spiritual life.

Linger leisurely with each reflection. Allow the saints you will encounter here to take you on a pilgrimage of the interior life. Allow their wisdom to soak in, become a part of you, and change you. The goal is to allow God to shape your interior life and lead you to grow in trust, surrender, and holiness. Don't just learn about these themes. Let God write the themes of this spiritual pilgrimage on your heart.

So take your time with each reflection. Read it prayerfully. Pause when something moves you. Put the book down for a moment, and talk to God about what you just read. Write a note in the margin. Reflect on how an insight from a saint might apply to your life right now and how God might be encouraging you, challenging you, inviting you to go deeper in friendship with him. Pray about the question posed at the end of the reflection. Think of this book as a conversation starter of sorts, facilitating a personal conversation with the Lord.

The saints will be your guides. It's the wisdom of the saints that shapes each reflection. You will encounter the life and writings of various modern saints, like St. Teresa of Calcutta (Mother Teresa), St. Faustina, and St. John Paul II, as well as early Christian leaders like St. Augustine and St. Benedict. You'll also be inspired by the captivating humanness of medieval saints like St. Catherine of Siena, St. Thomas Aquinas, and St. Bernard of Clairvaux and later spiritual giants such as St. Ignatius of Loyola, St. John of the Cross, St. Teresa of Avila, St. Thérèse of Lisieux, and St. John Henry Newman. The saints and other well-known spiritual writers touch every page of this book and will help you on this journey.

"But the Saints Are Beyond Me!"

Sometimes, however, we can be intimidated when we hear stories about the saints. We learn about extraordinary events in their lives and put them on such a high pedestal that we forget they were human. We view the saints as spiritual superheroes who do amazing things like stay up all night in prayer, levitate, read people's souls, and fast for long periods of time. We admire their amazing love for God from afar, but in the end, we're not sure we can relate to them. We might say to ourselves, "I'm just an ordinary Catholic. I could never do all that. I don't have their spiritual superhero powers. I could never be as holy as they were."

But what if I were to tell you that the saints were human beings who struggled as we do—men and women who struggled in prayer, faced difficult problems, battled against many temptations, and even made mistakes? But each time they fell, they repented and got up again, entrusted themselves to God's mercy, and learned to rely ever more on God's grace to help them do what they could never do on their own. Pope Benedict XVI describes how encouraging it is to know that the saints faced the same kinds of challenges we often do: "Hence there are also disputes, disagreements and controversies among saints. And I find this very comforting, because we see that the saints have not 'fallen from heaven.' They are people like us, who also have complicated problems." Pope Benedict goes on to describe how the true holiness of the saints is not found in a kind of perfectionism—as if they never made mistakes. Their perfection often was forged through countless stumbles and setbacks, but they allowed God to meet them in their lowliness and carry them to heights in the spiritual life they could never have achieved on their own. Pope Benedict explains, "Holiness does not consist in never having erred or sinned. Holiness increases the capacity for conversion, for repentance, for willingness to start again and, especially, for reconciliation and forgiveness. ... It is not the fact that we have never erred but our capacity for reconciliation and forgiveness which makes us saints. And we can all learn this way of holiness."[1]

Indeed, this is a path to holiness that is not beyond any of us. It is within the reach of those who have been devout Christians most of their lives as well as those who are just starting to grow in their relationship with God. No matter what we have done in the past or how many imperfections we may have in the present, this kind of holiness is something we can all pursue. What God did in countless saints throughout the ages he wants to do in ordinary people like you and me: meet us in our weakness, wounds, and sins, and transform us with his grace. And that's what this book is all about: the spiritual journey God wants to take us on in prayer.

Your Itinerary

Our journey through key themes in Catholic spirituality begins in the first section (Reflections 1–5) by considering the essence of prayer itself: what the *Catechism of the Catholic Church* calls "the encounter of God's thirst with ours" (CCC 2560). This theme in Mother Teresa's writings reminds us that prayer is not primarily about what we do and how we perform; rather, it is about encountering God's ardent desire for us, his thirst for our love, our attention, and our heart's surrender.

The next section (Reflections 6–9) addresses the various struggles we all face in prayer: dryness, distraction, discouragement, restlessness, and the feeling that God is not close to us in prayer. St. Catherine of Siena sheds light on how God uses our difficulties in prayer to test our hearts, to test our faithfulness, and most of all to help us persevere through trials so we may be brought to a deeper level of love and intimacy.

The third and fourth sections (Reflections 10–14) delve into how, through prayer, God helps us grow in confidence in his plan for our lives and surrender ever more to his will. St. Faustina, St. Ignatius of Loyola, and St. John Paul II invite us to put all our trust in Jesus, to abandon everything to him and "open wide the doors for Christ," allowing ourselves to be led by the Lord each day, using our lives for God's purposes and not our own.

The fifth section (Reflections 15–20) addresses our struggles with sin and weakness. Though our imperfections can be discouraging, St. Thérèse of Lisieux reminds us that God wants to meet us in our poverty, as we are, with our many faults and blemishes—not in spite of them—so that we can receive his love at a deeper level. We will see that the first significant step in the spiritual life is the foundational step downward into what Thérèse calls "the valley of humility."

The sixth section (Reflections 21–26) focuses on the healing of our emotions, desires, wounds, and attachments. Indeed, our sins, addictions, disordered desires, out-of-control emotions, hurts from the past, and false stories we tell ourselves all handicap us, making it harder for us to receive God's love and share it with others. But as we will see, especially through the writings of St. John of the Cross, God wants to touch every aspect of our personalities, healing and conforming them to Christ's image.

The seventh part (Reflections 27–28) helps us live deeply with Jesus amid the ubiquitous noise in the modern age. The frantic pace of our days and the alluring images, voices, and lifestyles that surround us hinder many good Christians from going deeper in the spiritual life. St. Benedict reminds us as Christians in our own non-Christian culture that we need to step back from the influences of the world and maintain a place within our souls where we can abide with Jesus. And we will see from St. John Henry Newman that we must be not conformed to this world but be transformed by the renewal of our minds (Romans 12:1–2).

The final section (Reflections 29–30) highlights one of the brightest marks of true holiness: love of neighbor. Jesus doesn't want to meet us just in the chapel; he also wants to meet us day to day in the people around us. Through prayer, God transforms our hearts so that we love the people in our lives—our spouse, our kids, our friends, the poor, and the suffering—as Christ loved us. Here, various medieval saints such as Bernard of Clairvaux and Francis of Assisi will be our primary guides.

Getting Started: The Thirty-Day Prayer Challenge

If we want the wisdom of the saints in this book to bear much fruit in our lives, we must build a consistent daily prayer life. Some of us might already have this habit. For others, however, the idea of regular prayer might be something new. Some of us might even be feeling a little unsure about prayer itself and wondering, "How do I pray? Practically, what do I do when I go to pray? I want to pray, but I'm not sure how to get started."

If you find yourself asking these questions, rest assured that God meets us wherever we are in our journey with him. He is the one who has given us that initial desire to pray, and he will help us take the first steps of growing in a consistent prayer life. To help you get started, I have provided a short practical guide on prayer in the appendix, called "How to Pray." It is based on the Church's teachings on prayer and the Catholic spiritual tradition. Take a moment to read this simple guide, which provides practical tips on what to do during prayer and how to get started. Whether you're new to daily prayer or looking for a refresher to help you rekindle your prayer life, it is my hope that this short guide in the back of the book will help you with whatever next step God is inviting you to take in your journey with him in prayer.

But the most important part of cultivating the habit of prayer is consistency: taking fifteen, twenty, or thirty minutes every day for quiet time with the Lord in prayer. Making daily prayer a priority in our busy schedules is essential for growth in the spiritual life.

It is often said it takes at least thirty days to build a habit. So commit to taking time out for quiet prayer each day for thirty days. St. Ignatius of Loyola, the patron saint of retreats, is known for his famous thirty-day retreat called the Spiritual Exercises. While you may never be able to get away to do a full thirty-day silent retreat, you can commit to taking time for prayer each day for at least thirty days in a row. The thirty reflections in this book can be your guide. You can read one reflection prayerfully each day for thirty days to help nourish your conversation with God, ponder how the Lord may be speaking to you each day through the wisdom of the saints, and ask him how the various themes in these reflections apply to your life.

What's most important, however, is that you take time for prayer each day, not that you complete a whole reflection each day. You should not, therefore, force yourself to rush through a reflection simply to complete an entire reflection daily. Completing the reflections themselves is not the primary aim; daily conversation with God is. The reflections are there to nourish your prayer time, giving you something to meditate on and talk to God about. So while praying, if you find that you are moved by certain sections and want to ponder them longer, that's good! Feel free to linger on those sections and do not feel bad if you read only a small part each day. If you read only half a reflection each day, for example, that is not a problem. You can simply extend the thirty-day prayer challenge to however many days you need.

* * * * * *

I hope the wisdom of the saints contained in these thirty reflections will inspire you to pray more from the inside and cooperate more with God in prayer, yielding ever more of your life to him and his plan for you. May you have confidence that his love will transform you and guide you every step of the way in your lifelong pilgrimage of prayer.

Edward Sri

October 1, 2022

Feast of St. Thérèse of Lisieux

Part One

THE DIVINE FLAME WITHIN

1

"I Thirst"

When visiting a chapel of the Missionaries of Charity—the religious order Mother Teresa founded in 1947—one is immediately struck by the simplicity, indeed the austerity, of the sacred space. There are no chairs, pews, or kneelers. The sisters take off their shoes before entering the chapel and sit on the bare floor. The room is quiet, humble, unassuming. Typically, there are no ornate pieces of religious art. Just a gold tabernacle behind the altar, a statue of Mary in one corner and perhaps a statue of Jesus in the other.

There is one image, however, that immediately arrests one's attention: a large crucifix behind the altar with two stark words alongside it painted in large, black capital letters: I THIRST. All eyes are drawn to the cross and these two sacred words spoken by Jesus on the Cross: "I thirst" (John 19:28).

For Mother Teresa, these two words on the chapel wall served as a constant reminder of one of the most profound mysteries of God: *God's thirst*. She saw that when Jesus spoke the words "I thirst" from the Cross, he was referring to much more than a physical thirst for water. Jesus was crying out in thirst for souls. But here we must be clear: this was not just a thirst for souls in general, for the billions of souls out there in the world. What was somewhat unique in Mother Teresa's understanding of these words was that she saw that Jesus was crying out from the depths of his heart's ardent thirst for each person individually, personally: Jesus thirsts for *her* love, *her* time, *her* attention, *her* entire life.[2] She was in awe that the God of the Universe needed something *from her!* She described Jesus' "I thirst" as revealing "the depths of God's infinite longing to love and be loved."[3]

Have you ever pondered that amazing truth—that God is longing to be loved by *you*, yearning for your time and attention, thirsting for you to give him your entire heart?

This idea of God's infinite thirst for her love was at the center of Mother Teresa's entire spirituality. It was the reason she founded the Missionaries of Charity sisters, and it was a constant source of wonder for her. On one occasion, in a conversation at the Mother House in Calcutta, she expressed her overwhelming awe over God's thirst for her, indeed, his *need* for her, saying, "That God is high, transcendent, all-powerful, almighty, I can understand that because I am so small. But that God has become small, and that he thirsts for my love, *begs* for it—I *cannot* understand it, I *cannot* understand it, I *cannot* understand it!"[4]

Making "I Thirst" Personal

What specifically is Jesus thirsting for in us? He longs for our love—our attention, our ardent devotion, the total entrusting of our lives to him. Reflecting on Jesus' words from the Cross, Mother Teresa said, "At this most difficult time He proclaimed, 'I thirst.' And people thought He was thirsty in an ordinary way and they gave Him vinegar straight away; but it was not for that thirst; it was for our love, our affection, that intimate attachment to him, and that sharing of His Passion. He used, 'I thirst,' instead of 'Give Me your love' ... 'I thirst.' Let us hear Him saying it to me and saying it to you."[5]

Mother Teresa made Jesus' statement "I thirst" so personal that she told her sisters to imagine Jesus saying those words directly to each of them, individually, personally. She even encouraged them to put their own name before the words "I thirst" and hear Jesus saying, for example, "Sister Mary Vincent, I thirst."

We can do the same. We can put ourselves in the silent presence of God, in a quiet place at home or in front of the Blessed Sacrament, and prayerfully imagine Jesus gently calling our name and speaking these two words to each of us—like this: "Edward, I thirst." Mother Teresa says, "Just put yourself in front of the tabernacle. Don't let anything disturb you. Hear your own name and 'I Thirst.' I thirst for purity, I thirst for poverty, I thirst for obedience, I thirst for that wholehearted love, I thirst for that total surrender. Are we living a deeply contemplative life? He thirsts for that total surrender."[6]

Yes, that is what Jesus is thirsting for: our hearts, our entire lives, our entrusting of everything into his hands. Many of us, however, hold back. We are afraid to surrender ourselves to him in this way. Though a part of us may want to give more of ourselves to God, another part fears letting go of control and remains clinging to our own plans. Meanwhile, Jesus waits for our response as he continuously says to us, "I thirst."

Do you desire to give your life more to God, to trust him more, to use your life for his purposes and not your own? Do you desire to respond with all your heart to Jesus' thirst for your love? It is in prayer that our hearts are healed, molded by the Lord, and gradually changed. It is in prayer, more than anywhere else, that we become the kind of people who respond to Christ's thirst for our love. Indeed, for those who genuinely desire to grow in the spiritual life, those words of Jesus on the Cross—"I thirst"—bring us to the very heart of prayer.

The Heart of Prayer

If you have ever felt uncertain about what to do during prayer or that you are not very good at praying, you are in good company. Most of the saints felt that way at one time or another, and some, like Mother Teresa, for large parts of their lives. From the very beginning of Christianity, those who have sincerely loved the Lord have found prayer to be challenging at times, difficult, dry, or even painful.

Take, for example, St. Paul—the one who had visions of God, who zealously spread the Gospel around the Roman world, who wrote most of the New Testament books, and who gave up his life as a martyr for the Faith. Even the great St. Paul admitted that "we do not know how to pray as we ought" (Romans 8:26). So if you ever have moments when you feel like you don't know what you are doing in prayer, remember the Apostle Paul and the thousands of other saints who also experienced various struggles in prayer. God met them in those struggles and transformed them over time. He can do the same with you.

Part of the problem might be how we view prayer primarily as something we *do*—an important spiritual activity and one we must carry out very well. The focus is on our end, on how we perform, on how well we say our prayers: Am I using the right method, saying the right words, reading the right book for prayer? Am I attentive enough, concentrating enough, putting my heart enough into prayer? Prayer, however, is not about my performance. Even less is it simply a box to check off—a spiritual chore to fit into my busy schedule. "Good, I got my prayer in today."

While faithfulness to daily prayer and coming to prayer with the right dispositions are absolutely crucial, Mother Teresa's devotion to the thirst of Jesus reminds us that prayer is primarily *God's* work, not ours. *The fact that you desire to pray is itself a sign of God already working in you. He put that desire in your heart.* It is God who takes the initiative, who wants this relationship with us even more than we do. It's up to us to respond to his love, to make space for him to work in our hearts and cooperate with him in what he wants to do in our souls. And Jesus is longing, begging, thirsting for us to let him in, to give him that time and attention, that interior space. As Mother Teresa once said, "He longs for you. He misses you when you don't come close. He thirsts for you."[7]

That's how we should view prayer. Not merely as some obligation to fulfill, an item to check off the list. That's not the Catholic view of prayer. Prayer ultimately is "a response of love to the thirst of the only Son of God" (CCC 2561). *Will you make time each day to really meet him in prayer? Will you respond to God's love for you—his thirst for you—with your whole being, your entire life, and most especially in prayer?*

* * * * * *

Prayerfully imagine yourself at the foot of the Cross with Jesus on Good Friday. He gazes on you with love, calling your name and saying, "[Your name], I thirst." How would you respond?

2

The Meeting of Two Desires

The story of Jesus meeting the Samaritan woman at the well would have been utterly shocking for Jews in the first century (see John 4:1–42). Since the Samaritan people were considered sinners who broke away from God's People, Jesus talking to a Samaritan woman would have been frowned upon. Moreover, this particular woman would have been considered a great sinner, for she had had five different husbands and was currently living with another man. As the details of her life unfold, many ancient Jews would wonder, "Why would Jesus spend time with a woman like this?"

Nevertheless, Jesus seeks her out. It's as if he has an urgent need to be near her. He goes out of his way to travel to Samaria, enters her village, and waits at the well. When she shows up, *he's* the one to initiate the conversation. And his first words to this woman are not "Repent!" or "Get your act together!" Nor does he start off teaching her how he is the Lord of the Universe and how she needs him for her salvation. Instead, Jesus says the most unexpected thing. The Divine Son of God surprisingly expresses *his* need for something *from her*! He says, "Give me a drink" (John 4:7). It is as if Jesus's whole point in coming to this village is to tell this woman about some pressing need he has: his thirst.

The story is a beautiful analogy for our relationship with God in prayer. We are like the Samaritan woman, and Jesus stands before us today, looking us in the eye, saying, "Give me a drink." God is not coming like a powerful master, merely demanding that we worship him and give him time for prayer. The God of the Universe approaches us humbly, like a lover, as if he *needs* something from us, and like a beggar, pleads for our hearts. He thirsts not for water but for our love, our attention, our entire heart, just as Mother Teresa experienced. He longs for us to meet him in prayer each day. He rejoices when he sees us prioritizing time for prayer in our busy schedules, taking time to be with him each day. As the *Catechism* explains, "It is he who first seeks us and asks us for a drink. Jesus thirsts; his asking arises from the depths of God's desire for us. Whether we realize it or not, prayer is the encounter of God's thirst with ours. God thirsts that we may thirst for him" (CCC 2560).

The fourteenth-century mystic St. Catherine of Siena made a similar point. When she thought about prayer, she focused less on her own performance in prayer and more on God's role and his desire for us. In fact, she taught that God loves us so much that, when he created us, he placed a longing in our hearts for him. Indeed, God created human persons with infinite longings that only he, the Infinite One, can fulfill.[8]

Let's stop and ponder this important point for a moment: When God brought you into existence, he placed an infinite desire in your heart that only he could satisfy. The God who is love desires to be united with you and is constantly appealing to those deepest desires he placed in your heart, inviting you to turn more to him and away from anything that distracts you from his love. He is constantly drawing you to seek him who alone can fulfill you.

For St. Catherine of Siena, this is the very essence of prayer: the uniting of these two infinite desires, God's infinite desire for us and our infinite desire for him. Here, Catherine offers one of the simplest and yet most profound descriptions of prayer: "It is the desire of God which draws to itself the desire that is in the depths

of the soul, in such a way that together they make one thing."[9]
Think about what that means. *Prayer is not simply something you do.
It's the place of encounter. It's where God, who so ardently desires to be
united with you, draws out of you the deepest desires of your soul—the
desires he put there!—and draws you ever closer to himself.*

* * * * * *

*Like the Samaritan woman, meet Jesus at the well in your prayer,
remembering that he thirsts for us to thirst for him. He thirsts
for our time, our attention, our love, our surrendering our lives
entirely to him. Ask him to show you an area of your life that he
thirsts for most right now, that he thirsts for you to give to him.*

3

The Primacy of Your Interior Life

Do you take time each day for prayer? The soul needs prayer like the body needs oxygen. To be filled more with Christ's life, we need to take in what Pope Francis called "the deep breath of prayer."[10]

In this reflection, we're going to discuss something very important. We're going to cover some basics about how crucial the habit of daily prayer is. For some of you, this reflection will simply encourage you to persevere in daily prayer. For others, it will be new, challenging, and I hope inspiring. But for *all* of us, we need to visit again and again these basic points about daily prayer because they are so foundational. If we wish to continue moving forward in friendship with the Lord, we must always be cultivating an ever deeper interior life. Otherwise, we risk becoming the kind of Christians who "lose their first love" (Revelation 2:4), becoming stagnant in the spiritual life, or getting stuck merely going through the motions of our faith. We might believe, say, and do the right things, but are we truly being led by the Spirit and transformed into Christ's likeness at the deepest levels? If we wish to encounter God in the deep caverns of our souls, we must continually renew our commitment to daily prayer.

But here we must be clear. By daily prayer we should be thinking of more than reciting vocal prayers, such as the Our Father, Hail Mary, or grace before meals. We should also have in mind something more than certain devotions such as the Rosary or the Divine Mercy chaplet or the liturgical prayers of the Church such as Morning and Evening Prayer. The deep breath of prayer entails even more than the Mass, which is the highest form of prayer.

Do you take time each day to cultivate a deep interior life? Do you take time—fifteen, twenty, or thirty minutes a day—for intimate conversation with the Lord, talking to him as a friend? The heartbeat of our spiritual lives should be the daily encounter with the Lord in what the Church calls "meditation," which involves reflecting on Christ's life and conversing with God about how to live ever more according to his plan. This can be done by meditating on the Scriptures using traditional approaches such as *lectio divina* or Ignatian contemplation. Some Christians also use classical spiritual books such as Thomas a Kempis' *Imitation of Christ*, or St. Francis de Sales' *Introduction to the Devout Life*. Others use modern resources such as *In Conversation with God, My Daily Bread,* or the reflections in *Magnificat*. These works help us contemplate God and his plan for us, and they invite us to reflect on how we can encounter him more in our daily lives and live more like Christ.

Whatever method or tool you employ, the important thing for every Christian is to have time set aside each day for conversation with the Lord. We can allow him to speak to us through Scripture or the saints. We can read a line or two from a sacred text and then pause to reflect prayerfully on those lines and talk to God about how they might apply to our life. In this process of reading, reflecting, and talking to God about our meditation, we might find ourselves inspired to tell him we love him or thank him for his goodness. We might sense God comforting or encouraging us in a certain trial we're facing. We might have a better sense of God leading us in a certain direction, prompting us to make a sacrifice or challenging us to make a change, repent, and say sorry for a way we've failed to love as we should. (For more practical tips on what to do in prayer, see the "How to Pray" guide in the appendix.)

Mass or Meditation?

But some might wonder if this kind of prayer is really necessary: "I listen to Catholic podcasts, Catholic radio, and prayers on Catholic apps—isn't that enough to feed my spiritual life. Isn't saying the Rosary each day enough? Or saying novenas? Or reciting the psalms in the Liturgy of the Hours? Many people in today's world don't even pray; I, at least, take some time to recite prayers like these!" If you are doing those forms of prayer, keep doing them. If you're not, consider incorporating them into your spiritual life at some point. They can enrich your spiritual life in important ways. But they won't bear as much fruit in your life if you don't have a commitment to daily conversation with the Lord in prayer.

Still others might object: "But what about the Mass? The Mass is the highest form of prayer! If I have to choose between going to a weekday Mass or getting quiet meditative prayer in during the week, shouldn't I choose Mass?"

But that's not the best question to ask.

Yes, the Mass is, indeed, the highest form of prayer. It is Christ's sacrificial offering of himself to the Father—the greatest act of worship ever—made present for us at every Mass. And yet, if we don't have a deep interior life, the real graces we receive in the Eucharist may not bear as much fruit. We need both. Holy Communion and holy conversation with the Lord work hand in hand.

So the question "Should I go to a daily Mass or take time for prayer?" is not a good question.* It's almost like in a marriage, asking, "If I am very busy and have to choose between having marital relations with my spouse or talking with my spouse, which one should I choose?" That's a bad question! The marital act is the most intimate *physical* expression of love a husband and wife can share together. Their bodily union in sexual intimacy is meant

---

*Here we continue to refer to weekday Masses. Of course, Sunday Mass and Masses for Holy Days of Obligation must always be fulfilled.

to express a profound *personal* union, indeed, a deeper spiritual union. Ideally, the sexual act expresses physically what already exists heart-to-heart between husband and wife and helps deepen that union further. But if, for example, a man neglects talking with his wife regularly—if he's too busy and doesn't have time for real conversation with her to know what is on her heart—then the marital act may become more about bodily union and less about personal union. It may not deepen the relationship as it is intended to do and instead become just an act of physical pleasure.

Similarly, Mass without a daily prayer life is not going to be as fruitful in deepening our friendship with God. As Fr. Jacques Philippe explains,

> One may object that God bestows sanctifying grace on us and does so principally through the sacraments. Moreover, the Mass in itself is more important than personal prayer. This may be true, but without a prayer life, the sacraments would have a limited effect. The sacraments confer grace, but their effects are stunted because they do not find "good soil" in which to take root. We can ask ourselves, for example, why those who frequently receive Holy Communion are not holier. Often the reason is the absence of prayer in their life. The Holy Eucharist does not effect within the soul the healing and fruits it should because it is not welcomed with ardent faith, love, and adoration. ... Those who do not pray habitually, no matter how faith-filled or pious, will not achieve full spiritual maturity.[11]

Do you want the graces of the Mass and the sacraments to bear more fruit in your life? Then, be faithful to daily prayer so that those graces meet the fertile soil of a cultivated interior life.

* * * * * *

Ask Jesus how he's inviting you to spend concrete time in conversation with him each day. Make a commitment to him, as you would to a friend, to show up for that specific time each day. And ask him how he might be inviting you to give more of yourself to him during that time of prayer.

4

Faithfulness over Feelings

One thing that might keep us from a consistent prayer life is a focus on feelings—the feelings of comfort, encouragement, and closeness with God we might experience in prayer.

When people say they have a good time in prayer—"Prayer was good today"—they often mean they felt close to God in prayer. Perhaps they received some consolations, felt God's peace, sensed God's presence, experienced his love, or got some good insights on their life. These are beautiful blessings that the Lord sometimes bestows on a soul in prayer. They can encourage us and draw us closer to him at the well of prayer. We should thank the Lord for these gifts. But they are not the heart of prayer. And they certainly should not be interpreted as a sign of special holiness or growth in prayer. Nor should they be the main motivation for coming to prayer each day.

Feelings come and go in prayer. That's why *faithfulness* to prayer is far more important than any *feelings* we might receive in prayer. It is easy to persevere in prayer when we are receiving consolations or are feeling excited to pray, but it's more important to remain consistent when prayer is dry, boring, and inconvenient and we find ourselves incessantly restless or distracted in prayer. Faithfulness to prayer, especially when prayer is difficult, is a far more important act of love than any feelings, consolations, or deep spiritual thoughts we experience during prayer.

The key question is this: Are we loyal to Jesus even when it does not *feel* like good prayer, even when we *feel* like we're not getting any "feedback" from God or getting much out of our prayer time? Are we coming to prayer only for what we get out of it—the feelings—or are we showing up for prayer faithfully each day out of love for our Lord, to give ourselves to him and to give him the praise, thanksgiving, love, and attention that he justly deserves?

After all, real love is not all about feelings. My heart, for example, might be very moved when my three-year-old is so excited to see me when I come home. She sometimes runs to the door with a big smile on her face, saying, "Dadda home! Dadda home!" In those moments, I have such affection for her and just want to hug her! It feels great to be a dad in times like that.

But when that same three-year-old is waking us up every night at two o'clock for several weeks in a row, wanting a drink, wanting something to eat, or insisting she jump in our bed, I don't have those same feelings. (I *do* have feelings in those moments, but sadly, they're the kind of feelings I sometimes need to bring to Confession!) And yet I still need to be faithful to her—to help her, to serve her, to love her—even when the warm feelings are not there. Love is not about feelings. It's an act of the will, a decision, a commitment.

Similarly, when we don't have a feeling of God's closeness in prayer, will we still show up? Will we still be faithful? For as with any relationship of love, faithfulness day in and day out is much more important than the feelings one experiences in prayer. As Fr. Philippe explains, "It is not as important to experience moments of prayer that are beautiful and satisfying, rich in profound thoughts or sentiments, as it is to be faithful and persevering in prayer. In other words, we must not focus so much on the 'quality' but on our fidelity to prayer. Quality will be the fruit of fidelity.

Times of arid, impoverished, distracted, or relatively brief prayer, if practiced faithfully every day, are more meritorious and bear more fruit than long, ardent prayers offered inconsistently when we feel the circumstances conducive."[12]

Indeed, dryness in prayer is usually not a punishment from God. It is his gift to us. He gives us the opportunity to express our love in a new and powerful way. When we don't have feelings in prayer but still make an act of the will and commit ourselves to pray, Jesus, the angels, and the saints rejoice all the more, seeing our sacrificial faithfulness to the Lord. For in our heart is a selfless love that is so clearly about faithfulness to him for who he is and not for what he gives us in prayer.

"I Don't Have Time"

But some people say, "I'm too busy to make time for prayer each day. I have too much going on. I don't have time." In reality, we all have time. Everyone gets twenty-four hours each day. The question is, what we are doing with our time? Do we spend our time in a way that shows how much we value God, how much we want to give him the worship that is his due, how much we realize we need him and how much we love him?

Consider Jesus' words "Apart from me, you can do nothing" (John 15:5). Are we convinced of these words? Do we really believe we can do nothing apart from Jesus? Notice that he doesn't say, "Apart from me, you can only do about 50 percent." He says "nothing." And this is a fundamental truth we must keep before our minds: at every moment, God holds our entire existence in the palm of his hands—every breath, every movement, every thought, every action. All we do in the office and in our careers. All our friendships. Our family life. Our mission. All we do is dependent on God. It's not simply that, apart from Jesus, our projects, relationships, and activities in life will suffer. Apart from the Lord, we would cease to exist!

If we are truly certain of this truth, if we humbly recognize how much we are really dependent on God for all we do, we certainly would make time to rely on him and draw on his guidance and strength each day in prayer. As I've written in another work,

> If we were humbly convinced of our nothingness, of how much we really need God, of how little we could do without him, we would be rushing to the chapel regularly, stopping in the middle of our day to tell him we love him, to ask for his guidance, and to beg for his help. We would make the time for prayer in our daily lives. But someone who claims to be too busy for prayer subtly thinks he can actually get by in life on his own—in his job, family, moral life, and Christian living. Jesus wants to meet you each day in prayer. He is thirsting for you at the well. Will you take time to meet him in prayer?[13]

When we neglect fitting prayer into our busy schedules, however, we may be suffering from a deeper problem—not busyness but a problem of the heart: "For where your treasure is, there will your heart be also" (Matthew 6:21; Luke 12:34). Living day to day without consistent prayer may be an indication of a heart that has lost its first love (see Revelation 2:4), a heart that does not value God as much as it should. It may also point to a certain spiritual pride, not recognizing how dependent we are on God for everything in our lives. For when we don't make prayer a priority each day, it's as if we are saying, "I've got this, God. I can do this. I don't need you."

People don't die of starvation because they were too busy and didn't have time to take a meal. ("Poor guy. He was just so busy, had so much going on at work and at home. He didn't have time to eat.") No. We make time for activities we consider vital. The question is, do we see time with God as essential for our spiritual life, for all we do and all we are? Just as we need to breathe in oxygen moment by moment, do we see it as absolutely critical to take in "the deep breath of prayer" each day?

* * * * * *

Have there been times when you felt close to God in prayer? If so, thank the Lord for those blessings. Have there been times when prayer was difficult and you did not feel close to God in prayer? How did you respond? Did you remain faithful to daily prayer despite the lack of feelings in prayer? Or did you allow yourself to fall into frustration, discouragement, or even cutting back on your time in prayer? Talk to God about your challenges in prayer.

5

Radiating Christ

We're not the only ones who benefit from our faithfulness to daily prayer. The people around us are depending on us to pray every day. When we do not have a deep interior life, our spouse, children, friends, coworkers, and family will suffer. We will not be able to give the best of ourselves to them. We will tend to live more superficially, relying on our own personality, talents, and abilities instead of allowing God to work more profoundly through us to love and serve the people in our lives.

I know that my wife and children, for example, need a lot more than my human love for them. They need Christ loving them through me. I do sincerely love my family. And my love for them has some noble qualities. But I also know my love is tainted by my own pride, selfishness, weakness, wounds, and sin. My wife and children need more than what I can give them on my own. They need Christ's love supernaturally working through me.

How about you? Consider the people at work, in your parish, and in your community—the people you serve: do you give them more than merely your own personal skills, talent, wisdom, leadership abilities, and charming personality? We should use all our humanity, of course, to give the best of ourselves to others in all we do. But the best of ourselves, actually, is *more* than ourselves. It is Christ radiating through us.

How about your family, your spouse, your closest friends—do the people in your life encounter something in you bigger than you are? Do they encounter Jesus Christ radiating through you? Only when we live from the depths of our interior lives do our friendships, families, work, and mission become infused with a greater love that the world has not known, the love of Christ.

Mother Teresa emphasized this point with her Missionary of Charity sisters throughout the world. Every morning, before they go out to the slums to serve the poorest of the poor, the sisters do a Holy Hour of prayer before the Blessed Sacrament and then receive Holy Communion at Mass. After Mass, they recite a prayer that contains this beautiful petition to Jesus: "Shine through us, and be so in us, that every soul we come in contact with may feel your presence in our soul. Let them look up and see no longer us but only Jesus."[14]

What a remarkable prayer! *"Let them look up and see no longer us but only Jesus."* Wouldn't it be wonderful if every soul we came in contact with each day—our spouse, our children, our friends, our colleagues at work, the people in the parish, the poor on the street— if every person we met each day looked up and saw "no longer me but only Jesus"? If we wish to truly radiate Christ in this world, we must be committed to daily prayer.

There was a season in my life when my wife's commitment to prayer each morning interestingly began with making coffee the previous night. Before going to bed, she made a cup of coffee, put it in a thermos to keep it warm overnight, and put the thermos by her bedside. When she woke up in the morning, she could sit in our room, sip her coffee, and be fully awake for her morning prayer time with the Lord.

But why did she make her coffee the night before? Why not make a fresh cup in the morning? Because in our family of eight children, she knew that if she went to the kitchen to brew some coffee in the morning, she might never make it back to the quiet sanctuary of our bedroom for her prayer time. "Mom, where are my shoes?" "Can you sign this for school?" "I don't know what to eat for breakfast." "Who's taking me to practice this afternoon?" She wanted to come downstairs ready to give the best of herself to our children, which means giving them much more than herself. In the words of Mother Teresa, she wanted them to "look up and see no longer me but only Jesus."

Avoiding Harm

St. John of the Cross also noted how when we are not faithful to daily prayer, we can cause harm to those around us. In his sixteenth-century Spain, there were some priests who were frantically busy doing many good Catholic things like preaching, leading retreats, and proclaiming the Gospel. But he was concerned that their apostolic work was not rooted in a deep interior life. They were not praying. John of the Cross said,

> Let those who go bustling about, who think they can transform the world with their exterior works and preaching, take note that they would profit the Church more and be far more pleasing to God … if they spent half as much time abiding with God in prayer. … Certainly, they would accomplish more and with less toil with one work than they would now with a thousand works thanks to their prayers and the increased spiritual strength from which they would benefit. Otherwise, their lives would be reduced to making a lot of noise and accomplishing little more than nothing, if not nothing at all, or indeed at times even doing harm. May God forbid that the salt should begin to lose its taste, since, even if it seems to produce some effect, in reality it would be good for nothing for it is certain that good works cannot be accomplished save with the grace of God.[15]

John's stinging words about the priests in his day can challenge us also. He is concerned that our many activities won't bear as much fruit for the kingdom without deep, consistent prayer. He also points out that, without a cultivated interior life, our many works might even do harm! Indeed, all that we do is impacted by our faithfulness or unfaithfulness to prayer. When we have a consistent prayer life, we are more likely to live from our interior life and have the Lord inspiring and guiding all our actions. When we fail to pray, however, all that we do is rooted in self: our projects at work, our efforts in raising our children, our spiritual activities, and our relationships. Without prayer, it's all primarily based on our own plans and efforts. And it may not even be what God wants. That's why John would say that without daily prayer, all that we do for our friendships, marriages, families, parishes, communities, and workplaces, not only might not bear as much fruit but we may even do them harm.

* * * * * *

*Pray the prayer called "Radiating Christ," which Mother Teresa
adapted from a prayer by St. John Henry Newman:*

Dear Jesus, help us to spread your fragrance everywhere we go.
Flood our souls with your spirit and life.

Penetrate and possess our whole being so utterly
that our lives may only be a radiance of yours.

Shine through us,
and be so in us,
that every soul we come in contact with
may feel your presence in our soul.

Let them look up and see no longer us
but only Jesus!

Stay with us,
and then we shall begin to shine as you shine,
so to shine as to be a light to others.

The light, O Jesus, will be all from you;
none of it will be ours.

It will be you, shining on others through us.

Let us thus praise you in the way you love best,
by shining on those around us.

Let us preach you without preaching,
not by words but by our example,
by the catching force,
the sympathetic influence of what we do,
the evident fullness of the love our hearts bear for you.[16]
Amen.

Part Two

STRUGGLES
IN
PRAYER

6

Restless, Distracted, and Dry: "Give God That Nothing"

Mother Teresa once told a priest these important words of advice. "If ... at the time of prayer or meditation it seems to you that not only have you been distracted in your prayer, but that you have done nothing at all, never leave that time or that place of prayer angry or bitter with yourself. First—turn to God and give God that *nothing!*"[17]

Mother Teresa here makes a beautiful point that offers much encouragement when we struggle in prayer. Even if we think we accomplish nothing in prayer, there is still something we can give to the Lord. The mere fact that we show up for prayer, that we take time for prayer, that we sincerely want to meet Jesus in prayer, is itself something beautiful we can give to God. Even if the prayer time itself does not go as well as we would like, we can still humbly offer our broken, imperfect prayer that feels like nothing. We can still "give God that nothing."

St. Thomas Aquinas explains that the intention to pray is the foundation of all prayer. When we make a good intention to pray—when we take time for prayer and sincerely strive to give the Lord the best of ourselves—that intention itself helps shape the goodness of our prayer time. According to Aquinas, "It is not necessary that prayer should be attentive throughout because the force of the original intention with which one sets about praying renders the whole prayer meritorious."[18] In this sense, having a good *intention* is more important than maintaining good *attention* during prayer. Even if we lose attention during prayer, as long as we began prayer with a good intention, our prayer is still an expression of our love for the Lord. It has value and is something the Father delights in.

When my little children bring me a bouquet of wilted dandelions from the yard, they're so excited to give their father a present. With big smiles and much enthusiasm, they hold out their hands and say, "Here Daddy, these are for *you!*"

What would you think if I got upset at them because the floppy dandelions are not nearly as beautiful as a bouquet of roses, or if I got angry with them for giving me wilted weeds? "Don't you realize these are weeds and not beautiful flowers? This is not the kind of gift you should give people! Don't ever try to give me a present again until you get it right!" No good father would respond that way. For me, it's ultimately not the actual present that matters. I see not just the dandelion. I see their hearts. I see how they are thinking of me and wanting to give me a gift. It's in their loving hearts that I rejoice.

It's similar with the prayer you offer to God. Even when your prayer doesn't go well and it feels like all you are giving God is a bunch of dandelions—you get distracted, your heart isn't into prayer, you fall asleep—as long as you take time for prayer and sincerely desire to give God your best, you are offering a beautiful gift to your Father. You must, of course, sincerely try to pay better attention, listen better, reflect on God's Word better in your prayer. But in the end, our Father in heaven doesn't just see the final product of your prayer ("You weren't attentive enough!") as if prayer were primarily about your performance. No, he sees your heart. He sees your good intention, even when you don't have laser-focused attention during prayer.

So the next time you find yourself distracted and restless and your heart is not fully engaged during prayer, remember that simply showing up for prayer and sincerely trying—simply being faithful each day—is the beginning of prayer and is itself a wonderful gift of our heart we give to God. As spiritual theologian Simon Tugwell explains, "It is not obligatory that our prayer should always be utterly recollected and fervent. ... What is essential is our intention to pray. It is not always possible to sustain attention, and fervor and devotion are unpredictable. ... It often happens that we go to Mass with a serious intention of engaging ourselves with the Liturgy, but then our attention wanders and our intention weakens; but the essential point is that *we are still there.*"[19]

Here's what you can do if your time in prayer turns out to be somewhat of a mess: you can still offer it to the Lord with your good intention: "Lord, I really wanted to be present to you in prayer. I'm sorry I was so distracted and my heart wasn't in it today. I am weak and humbly admit I'm not that good at prayer. I entrust even this muddled time in prayer to you and your mercy, trusting you see my heart and my desire for you. And I will continue to strive to give my attention more to you next time and trust in your grace to help me in whatever way and at whatever time you think best for my soul." Indeed, the next time you feel like you've accomplished nothing in prayer, remember Mother Teresa's advice: you can still "give God that nothing!"

* * * * * *

Offer a childlike prayer to God: "Father, I want to give you my best! But sometimes I can only give you 'wilted dandelions' in my prayer. Today I gather up every past difficult experience of prayer, those times when I feel like I've accomplished nothing. I gather them into a bouquet of wilted dandelions for you, trusting that you see my heart and my sincere desire to give myself to you in prayer. Even though it feels like nothing, here is my nothing! Amen."

7

Discouragement:
The Devil's Attack

But *why* is prayer so often a struggle? We love God and want to pray well. God himself wants us to pray. Prayer is good for us. Shouldn't it be a lot easier? Yet we sometimes don't feel close to God in prayer. We're distracted, thinking about what's for dinner, problems at work, problems at home, something someone said to us earlier in the day. Our minds are wandering in a million directions during prayer but too often not toward God.

Sometimes we're just restless in prayer, agitated, wishing we were somewhere else. We have a lot going on in life and are eager for the prayer time to end so we can move on to the next urgent thing.

Many times, we just don't feel close to God in prayer. We don't sense his presence. Is he really there? Or perhaps we're bored and falling asleep. Though some Christians talk about having beautiful holy thoughts during prayer, that's not our experience. We might, therefore, be tempted to tell ourselves, "I must be very bad at this prayer thing. Why should I bother to keep trying?"

Experiencing struggles in prayer is a normal part of the ebb and flow of one's interior life. There can be many reasons why someone doesn't feel close to God in prayer.

It could be because of a sin problem, a certain willfulness in serious sin or a stubbornness in not truly being open to God's plan for your life. It's important that we consider this possibility. This is, of course, different from someone who falls into sin but recognizes that what he did was wrong, feels bad, repents, brings it to Confession, and sincerely tries to do better next time. God always bestows his mercy upon us when we come to him humbly in our weakness and he sees our contrite hearts.

But there are some Christians who willfully do sinful things, and instead of repenting, they rationalize their sin and don't think they need to change. "God doesn't mind what I do on the weekend. Everyone else does this. Everyone else watches this show. This isn't a big deal. I'm still a good person. I don't need to change." When we put ourselves into sin and stubbornly try to justify our actions instead of repenting, we put roadblocks in our friendship with God that inhibit our growth in prayer and the spiritual life.

In these situations, we also probably don't feel comfortable being *too close* to God. We keep a little distance, holding back because we're afraid of being too vulnerable with him in prayer—we don't want God to challenge us or call us to give up something. We don't want to change our behavior, admit we were wrong, or do something different. We tell ourselves, perhaps even subconsciously, that it is safer to avoid sincerely opening our hearts wide to God in prayer than it is to face him as he calls us to repent.

But struggles in prayer more often have nothing to do with a persistent sin problem. And here, the writings of St. Catherine can be very helpful, as she explains there can be several other reasons for these common trials in prayer that point either to the devil's discouraging us or to God's beautiful working in our souls.

The Devil's Attack

First, the dryness or struggles in prayer might, for example, be the devil rattling us, discouraging us, getting us to think we're not good at prayer, that we don't get a lot out of prayer, that we shouldn't bother with prayer. Do you ever have those thoughts? "You stink at prayer. You never pay attention. Your prayer is not pleasing to God. You don't have time for prayer. It's lonely. It's boring! You don't get anything out of it. It doesn't make a difference for your life." Those voices are not from God. They come from the enemy. The devil wants to discourage you, to make you think your prayer is worthless. He knows how powerful daily prayer is for the Christian life, and he'll use anything to get you to break your faithfulness to it. He even will play upon the Christian's noble desire to have a good prayer life and the humble sadness that comes when prayer does not seem to be going well. When a person notices that she is struggling in prayer, the devil pounces on that and tries to make "the soul feel that her prayer is not pleasing to God" and give up.[20] Such discouragement, however, is never from God.

St. Catherine says when a soul is disheartened by the state of its prayer life, the most important thing to do is to persevere. Never give up, she says. Find the courage to resist the temptation to quit. Remember who it is that is troubling you and discouraging you. Remember that the devil is trying to get you to compromise your commitment to daily prayer. The best way to fight back is by resolving to persevere in faithfulness each day.

"I Pretend Not to Hear Your Prayers"

Second, another reason we might be experiencing dryness in prayer is that God is testing our hearts. He is testing us to see what we will do if we don't receive feelings and consolations during prayer: *will we still come to him?*

God wants to take our love for him to the next level. He wants to transform it to a more perfect, self-giving love. One way he does this is, surprisingly, by taking away from us the very feelings and consolations he sometimes uses to encourage us in prayer. As paradoxical as that might seem, it is the testament of countless saints. It is even what God himself once told St. Catherine of Siena.

In a remarkable statement, God said, in reference to her prayers, "Sometimes ... I pretend not to hear you."[21]

Why would God say that? Isn't God the loving Father who always hears our prayers and responds to our needs? Why would he sometimes pretend to ignore us in prayer? Isn't God supposed to be a good conversation partner in prayer?

In his dialogue with Catherine, God goes on to explain an important difference between the *feeling* of his presence in prayer and the *reality of his grace* working in prayer. We might have profound moments in prayer when we sense God's closeness. Maybe on a retreat, at a conference, at a particular moment praying in a chapel—we feel God's love, we sense him stirring our hearts, we delight in the feeling of being close to him and look forward to being with him again in prayer. But there are many times when prayer is nothing like that at all. Often, it can be rather humdrum. At times, it might feel like a chore, and we don't have any sense of his closeness. It might even feel like we're in complete darkness during prayer and we wonder where God is.

But that doesn't mean he's not really there, present in his grace, doing profound work in our souls. Our Faith reminds us of this truth—that by virtue of our baptism and our remaining in the state of grace, God is truly present in our souls, working in our lives. The saints, in fact, tell us that some of the most significant periods of spiritual growth come not when prayer is fun, delightful, and full of consolations but when we go through a spiritual desert, when prayer is dry, hard, and downright uncomfortable. How we respond in those seasons of aridity is often what separates souls who plateau in the spiritual life from those who allow the Lord to truly lead them through the darkness to a whole new level of intimacy. Whatever struggle or discomfort we may experience in prayer, it is crucial to remember the fundamental truth that God is still present, very present, and perhaps, indeed, uncomfortably present, even if we don't *feel* his grace. As God told St. Catherine, "Though I may take away their comfort, I do not take away grace."[22] But why does God sometimes withdraw the feelings of his closeness? He told Catherine it's because he is testing us. He is testing our hearts, our desires. Will we still persevere in prayer even if we don't receive consolations?[23] Are we truly coming for him and him alone or do we come to him more for what we like to get out of prayer (help with my problems, peace, feelings of God's closeness, a sense of Him guiding my life, etc.)? These questions get to the central difference between an imperfect love and a more perfect love, an imperfect prayer and a more perfect prayer.

* * * * * *

What discourages you in prayer? Do you tend to come to your prayer expecting to get something out of it, or do you come for God himself? Take a moment to consider this question. Ask Jesus to help you love him for his own sake, not what he gives you in prayer, and surrender your prayer life to him.

8

"A Lover's Game"

The love between spouses is tested most when the marriage goes through difficult seasons—when the feelings fade and all that's left is a raw commitment to the beloved for his or her own sake.

Something similar happens in our relationship with God. Our beloved Jesus, our Bridegroom, often woos beginners to prayer by enriching it with his sweetness. When we first embark on cultivating an interior life, God might make various spiritual practices delightful for us. Whether it's retreats, Bible study, Eucharistic Adoration, spiritual reading, or prayer itself, it's all new, interesting, and exciting. Like a father holding out candy so his children come running into his arms, our heavenly Father might shower beginners with many delights in prayer to entice them to come back to him over and over again until the habit of prayer is more firmly established.

But God doesn't want to leave us as beginners. He eventually invites us to purify our love and go to the next level with him in prayer. He invites us to grow out of an imperfect love that is dependent on spiritual sweetness to reach a more perfect love that is directed to God himself. God told St. Catherine of Siena that the real test of one's love for God in prayer comes when the sweet consolations and feelings are no longer there. How will the soul respond?

There are [some people] who become faithful servants. ...
But their love is imperfect, for they serve me for their own
profit or for the delight and pleasure they find in me. Do you
know how they show that their love is imperfect? By the way
they act when they are deprived of the comfort they find in
me. And they love their neighbors with the same imperfect
love. This is why their love is not strong enough to last. No, it
becomes lax and often fails. It becomes lax toward me when
sometimes to exercise them in virtue and to lift them up out
of their imperfection, I take back my spiritual comfort and
let them experience struggles and vexations.[24]

This is important. When we experience darkness and trials in
prayer, we should not hit the panic button. We should not think
that God has abandoned us, that we have done something wrong,
or that we are simply incapable of prayer. The trials might be part
of God's inviting us to take the next step in the spiritual life, to
cultivate a more perfect love and trust him at a deeper level. As
God explains to Catherine, he sometimes *wants* us to experience
difficulties in prayer—not for the difficulties themselves but for
how those trials can heal our soul.

Drawn to a Deeper Love

One reason God withdraws good feelings in prayer is to help us
grow in humility. He explains to Catherine, "I do this to bring them
to perfect knowledge of themselves, so that they will know that
of themselves they have neither existence nor any grace."[25] When
we experience our poverty in prayer, when we acutely realize that
we don't really know what we're doing in prayer, it humbles us. It
makes us realize we don't have it all together. We come to a deeper
appreciation for how dependent we are on God to help us pray. We
call out to him more for help. And those are good things. God told
Catherine, "I want them, in time of conflict, to take refuge in me by

seeking me and knowing me as their benefactor, in true humility seeking me alone."[26]

This is why, at certain times in life, God might pretend to not hear our prayers. He wants to know our hearts. And he wants us to look inside our hearts and see what's really there. Do our hearts truly desire him and him alone? Or are we interested in prayer more for some insight or feeling we get out of it? By withdrawing the feeling of his closeness, he makes us long for him all the more. We come in deeper contact with the infinite desires on our souls which are for God alone.

As God explained to St. Catherine, he visits a soul in many different ways, not just with spiritual gladness. Sometimes his presence makes us contrite. Sometimes it troubles us as we grow in contempt for sin in our life. Sometimes God makes the truth of his Word known to the mind in a powerful way but without any feelings. Sometimes he is present and we don't feel anything. The feelings come and go, but God is always active, always working, always inviting us to grow in humility, patience, perseverance, and a more perfect love. As he tells Catherine, "I come and go, leaving in terms of feeling, not in terms of grace, and I do this to bring them to perfection. ... I call it a 'lover's game' because I go away for love and come back for love—no, not really I, for I am your unchanging and unchangeable God; what goes and comes back is the feeling my charity creates in the soul."[27]

So don't think of dryness as a punishment or as a sign that you are a failure at prayer. It's part of the lover's game. The God who is love is drawing you to a deeper love. God ultimately wants to draw out of your heart the deepest desires he placed there, which are not for consolations, feelings, or lofty spiritual thoughts. You were made for more than those good but less essential blessings in prayer. You were made for God himself. It is God himself for whom you ultimately hunger in prayer. As God explained to Catherine, "Sometimes, to test your desires and your perseverance, I pretend not to hear you. But I do hear you, and I give you whatever you need, for it is I who gave you the very hunger and voice with which you call me, and when I see your constancy, I fulfill your desires."[28]

How to Navigate the Desert

All this is part of his plan to lead us out of that imperfect love—the "spiritual selfishness" in which we love God for the consolations he gives us—to a more perfect love in which we love God for who he is. But what should we do in desert moments in prayer? God told Catherine never to get discouraged. The most important thing is to *persevere* in daily prayer, no matter how distracted, bored, or restless you are. Do not compromise. Do not lose heart. Do not compare yourself to other people and their experiences in prayer. Remember that simply intending to pray is itself a gift to the Lord.

Especially when you don't feel you're getting anything out of prayer, remember that your faithfulness to daily prayer is an all the more beautiful expression of your love for God—often more beautiful than when you receive much spiritual delight. As St. Faustina wrote, "One act of trust at such moments gives greater glory to God than whole hours passed in prayer filled with consolations."[29]

Also *be open to praying differently* than you're used to. Be patient and wait for the Lord. Sit quietly. Rest in the silence, solitude, and darkness. The author of *The Cloud of Unknowing* echoes this: "Learn to be at home in this darkness. Return to it as often as you can, letting your spirit cry out to him whom you love."[30] When sitting quietly in your arid, dry, empty prayer, you can humbly cry out to him, tell him of your pain, your bewilderment, your sadness. You also can tell him you love him. Tell him you miss him. In doing so, you might come into greater personal contact with something in the depths of your soul: your infinite desire for him. *Pay attention to those desires in your heart that long for a deeper union with him,* and allow God to draw out those desires that flow from the deep caverns of your soul.

* * * * * *

C. S. Lewis wrote, "If I find in myself a desire which no experience in this world can satisfy, the most probable explanation is that I was made for another world."[31] Take a moment and ask the Holy Spirit to help you to get in touch with the infinite desire on your soul—a desire only God can fulfill. Cry out to God from this place, asking him to fulfill those deepest desires of your soul.

9

Afraid of the Light

Little children are usually afraid of the dark. But I had one child who was afraid of the light.

We kept a small night-light in the boys' room that would turn on automatically whenever the overhead lights were off. While this had been a source of comfort for our other children, this one son freaked out whenever he saw the small light shining toward him through the darkness. He would have nothing to do with it and begged us to turn it off. He was afraid of that night-light and preferred to stay in the dark.

Sometimes we adults do the same. We prefer to stay in the dark. Prayer, real prayer, in which we allow God to come close and shine his light on us, can be uncomfortable. When God's light shines on our souls, we have to come to terms with our many imperfections. Yes, we might admit we have many sins and weaknesses. But it's one thing to say to ourselves and others, "I'm a sinner and have a lot of faults"—it's easy to check off that box and convince ourselves we have officially made it into the humility club. It's another thing to look inside ourselves and face the real truth about ourselves—the many fears, anxieties, wounds, hurts, insecurities, and dysfunctional defense mechanisms that keep us from going deeper in our relationships with others and with God; our pride, petty grudges and jealousies, anger, impure thoughts; our lack of trust, our desire to control everything, our constant scheming to get what we want instead of truly seeking God's will in our lives.

For some people, this kind of self-knowledge is scary. It's too uncomfortable to face the deep truth about ourselves. It's safer to remain in the dark and convince ourselves things are generally okay than it is to face the real truth about ourselves, that we actually don't have it together as much as we'd like to believe. Simon Tugwell once wrote, "While some of us are genuinely afraid of the dark, all of us are rather afraid of the light."[32]

And this is another reason we tend to avoid the quiet, daily prayer of meditation or contemplation. Other forms of prayer—like the Rosary, the Liturgy of the Hours, prayers we listen to on our devices or pray in a group—may feel safer to some people. Those forms of prayer let them people that they've accomplished something ("I got my Rosary done today. Check that one off the list!") and do not require them to be as vulnerable with the Lord. In quiet, meditative prayer, however, we sit silently with God with nothing but our own thoughts and desires. The silence, stillness, and solitude force us to come in touch with ourselves at a deeper level. We likely will experience our poverty, our restlessness, our inadequacy, our inability to pray well. We also might notice other things about ourselves that we'd rather not have to look at. God might shed light on a relationship we need to repair, a person we hurt and need to apologize to, a habit we need to get rid of, a sin we need to take to Confession, a pattern of behavior with others that he is challenging us to change. And that can be scary. When we enter deeper personal prayer, we realize how much we're not in control, how much we don't have it all together, and so we are afraid of going there. As Fr. Jacques Philippe explains,

> In the solitude and silence of personal prayer, we find ourselves face to face with God with nothing but our misery. It is difficult to accept our misery, and for this

reason we naturally tend to flee silence. In prayer, however, it is impossible to avoid feeling inadequate. Although we may often taste God's sweetness and tenderness in prayer, usually it is our wretchedness, inability to pray, concerns, distractions, the memory of old hurts, faults and failings, or our insecurities over the future that are all laid before our eyes. Thus, we find a thousand reasons to escape the stillness that unveils our radical nothingness before God. Indeed, we may refuse to accept our poverty and fragility.[33]

It's easier to do a hundred other things than it is to sit in the quiet of prayer for half an hour. It's much easier to respond to emails, check social media, go to a church event, or talk to a good Christian friend, than it is to sit in the silence of quiet, personal, meditative prayer. This is one reason we tend to avoid going deeper with God in prayer. We are all afraid of the light.

But even if it is initially scary, the Lord shining his light on my soul is what I most deeply want. "The LORD is my light and my salvation" (Psalm 27:1). In the quiet and solitude of prayer, God sheds light on our many fears, wounds, weaknesses, and sins not to shame or condemn us. He does it so he can begin to heal us. Jesus wants to fully enter our lives and heal whatever sins, attachments, and wounds keep us from flourishing in life, in our relationships, and most of all, in our friendship with him. The first step in this healing process is helping us become more aware of those problems and our need for God to help us. And that happens most profoundly in prayer—if we let him in.

* * * * * *

What is one place in your life where you've been afraid of the light? Offer that place to God in trust, asking him to shine his light there and begin to heal whatever fear, wound, or weakness might be keeping you from a deeper union with him.

Part Three

TRUST AND SURRENDER

10

Learning to Surrender

When St. Teresa of Calcutta started her religious order, the Missionaries of Charity, she didn't have a business plan, a marketing strategy, or the enthusiastic support of benefactors or Church leaders. It wasn't even her idea. It wasn't as if she looked out at the destitute on the streets of Calcutta and desired to start some new initiative to help them. This was not on her bucket list. The only reason she started the Missionaries of Charity was because she was answering a call from the Lord.

She had been serving happily for eighteen years as a missionary with the Sisters of Loretto, teaching the middle-class children in Calcutta. She enjoyed her work. She was making a difference. She liked her community. She was thriving.

But on September 10, 1946, Jesus called her to leave everything that was dear to her. He called her out of what was comfortable and into the unknown. While on a train ride to Darjeeling, India, in the foothills of the Himalayas, Mother Teresa heard the voice of Jesus calling her to start a new religious order dedicated to serving the poorest of the poor.

Up to this point in her life, she had already been very generous with the Lord. Growing up in Albania, she was inspired by stories of Jesuit missionaries who left Europe to evangelize in India. She chose to follow in their footsteps and gave up friends, family, and all that was familiar to her in order to become a missionary, too.

She joined the Loretto Sisters and went off to serve in far-off India, knowing she very likely would never see her loved ones again.

In those years as a Loretto sister, no one noticed anything extraordinary about her. She was a faithful, pious sister, a hard worker, and an effective teacher. What was most remarkable about her, however, could not be seen with human eyes, for it was hidden in the depths of her interior life. She was an extraordinary lover, determined to love Jesus with her whole heart and yearning to surrender her entire life to God. She was always looking for new ways to express her love. She wrote that, in those years, she had been "longing to be all for Jesus ... to love Him as he had never been loved before."[34] Indeed, while on a retreat in 1942, at the age of thirty-two, she resolved for the rest of her life never to refuse Jesus anything he asked of her: "Ask Jesus not to allow me to refuse Him anything, however small. I [would] rather die."[35]

That resolve was put to the test a few years later on the train to Darjeeling, when Jesus asked her to do the unthinkable: leave everything that was dear to her once again, step out into the unknown, and take on the difficult task of starting a new religious community focused not just on the poor but the poorest of the poor.

In the days and weeks following her "Inspiration Day," she continued to hear the insistent voice of Jesus asking her, "Wilt thou refuse?" Jesus was grateful for her generous love up to this point, but now, he was inviting her to take this next big step and surrender even more:

> You have become my Spouse for my Love—you have come to India for Me. The thirst you had for souls brought you so far—Are you afraid to take one more step for your Spouse—for Me—for souls?—Is your generosity grown cold?—Am I a second to you? You did not die for souls—that is why you don't care what happens to them.—Your heart was never

drowned in sorrow as was My Mother's. We both gave our all for souls—and you?[36]

These words are intense! Poor Mother Teresa! Imagine how she felt hearing this. The woman who had already given so much of her heart to Jesus is being pushed to give even more, to take this next, most daunting step of love and surrender.

Jesus then puts his finger on her deepest fear and makes her hesitate. It is not fear of the hard work in serving the poorest of the poor that makes her pause the most; it is her *fear of failure*. What if it doesn't work out? What if she doesn't have what it takes? What if she leaves her beloved Loretto sisters and her new religious community never takes off? She fears that if she fails in this new mission, she will no longer be able to be a religious sister and will have to become a lay person again. Jesus says to her,

> You are afraid that you will lose your vocation—you will become secular—you will be wanting in perseverance.—Nay—your vocation is to love and suffer and save souls and by taking this step you will fulfill my Heart's desire for you. ... You are I know the most incapable person, weak & sinful, but just because you are that I want to use you, for My glory! Wilt thou refuse?[37]

These words frightened Mother Teresa. In a letter to the Archbishop of Calcutta, she described how much she was afraid of stepping out into the unknown, afraid of failure and afraid of living the hard life of the poor people in India:

> The thought of eating, sleeping—living like the Indians filled me with fear. I prayed long—I prayed so much—I asked Our Mother Mary to ask Jesus to remove all this from me. The more I prayed—the clearer grew the voice in my heart and so I prayed that He would do with me whatever

He wanted. He asked again and again. Then once more the voice was very clear.[38]

This is what Jesus said in answer her prayer:

> You have been always saying "do with me whatever You wish."—Now I want to act—let me do it—My little spouse—My own little one.—Do not fear—I shall be with you always.—You will suffer and you suffer now. ... Let Me act.—Refuse Me not.—Trust Me lovingly—trust Me blindly. ... There are convents with numbers of nuns caring for the rich and able to do people, but for My very poor there is absolutely none. For them I long—them I love.—Wilt thou refuse?[39]

Mother Teresa's Yes

Have you ever told Jesus that you want to do his will? Have you ever prayed something like, "Jesus, please just show me your plan—make it clear what you want me to do—and I will do whatever you want"?

It's wonderful to say a prayer of surrender like this, to entrust our lives entirely into God's hands, to seek his will for our lives each day. But it is one thing to say a prayer like this. It is another thing to surrender and let Jesus act. On that fateful day in 1946, Mother Teresa gave the biggest yes of her life, surrendering her own plans and dreams and entrusting herself entirely to God's will, trusting that his plans are always so much bigger and better than anything we could come up with on our own.

But she could have said no. Mother Teresa could have refused Jesus, and no one would have noticed. She probably would have gone on living as a Loretto sister, teaching the children in India and doing some good work in her mission there. Everything on the outside would have looked the same. But something significant would have changed on the inside, something would have died, her wholehearted, generous love, her desire to surrender everything to God. And, as a result, the world would have been a very different place.

From Control to Surrender

Mother Teresa and all the other saints are the kind of people who seek to use their lives not for their own purposes but for God's. We all have been given free-will—we have the freedom to do whatever we want with our lives. But the saints are men and women driven by a burning love, and out of that love, they choose to give their freedom back to God as a gift. They choose to use their freedom to serve God's plan and not their own. Like a lover, Mother Teresa saw what was on God's heart—his desire for her to start the Missionaries of Charity—and even though it was going to be very difficult, she left everything behind to run after what her Beloved desired.

One of the things God wants to do in our prayer life is to turn our often fearful, controlling hearts into hearts of trust and surrender. In prayer, he teaches us to entrust more of ourselves to him like the saints did. This, however, requires total confidence in the God who loves us. Do we really believe the most basic truths of our Faith? That there is a God, he has a plan for our lives, and that plan is for our happiness? Do we really believe that God's plan, in fact, is better than anything we would come up with for ourselves? Do we really believe that giving up our own will to seek his will is what is truly best for us and ultimately will bring the lasting peace and fulfillment we desire?

It is one thing to agree intellectually with these fundamental truths of our Faith: "I know God is trustworthy, that he always provides for me, that he has an amazing plan for my life." It is another thing, however, to put that faith into practice and actually place our lives entirely in the Father's hands—to pray as Jesus himself prayed, "Not my will, but your will be done." God wants our hearts. He wants us to trust him with everything, holding nothing back.

And God doesn't want just *half* of our hearts. He doesn't want only 98 percent of our hearts. Remember, he is a lover who thirsts for us. He wants 100 percent of our hearts. Are we willing to give it all to him as Mother Teresa did? Or are we like the rich young man in the Gospel story (Luke 19), who outwardly follows all the commandments but inwardly clings to his many possessions and, because of them, won't give Jesus his whole heart or surrender everything to follow him?

Let us examine our consciences and ask ourselves, "Do I *truly* seek God's will for my life? Or do I focus more on my own will, what I want? Do I strive to become more a part of God's plans? Or do I merely invite God to help me with the schemes I have already decided for myself? Do I wake up each morning, thinking merely about what I want to do today, or do I ask the Lord how I can best serve him in my family, friends, work, and community? Do I seek him to guide all my decisions and inspire all my actions? In short, do I seek to use my life for his purposes or for my own?

Like the rich young man, we might have various "possessions" that keep us from going deeper in friendship with Jesus. We have things we're too attached to—a plan we have for our lives, something we think we absolutely need in order to be happy, a relationship, a job, a reputation, an achievement, a hope for our kids. Not all desires and hopes are evil, but if we are too attached to even the good and noble ones, they make it tougher for us to place all our hope in God. They weigh us down and prevent us from being truly led by the Lord.

Too often, we don't want to give up control. We don't want to make a change. We might give God parts of our lives, but we are afraid to entrust *everything* into his hands. We might *say* we will do whatever God wants, but in reality, we put parameters around God's will and limit how much we want him involved. We fear that if we let God fully in, he will mess with the precious dreams we have come up with for ourselves. Jesus knocks at the door of our hearts, but sometimes we are afraid to let him in *too* much.

* * * * * *

Even if you are afraid to let go of control of certain areas of your life, you can at least ask the Lord for the grace to help you surrender everything. Pray this beautiful prayer of surrender written by St. Ignatius of Loyola, expressing at least your desire to give God your entire life.

Take, Lord, and receive all my liberty,
my memory, my understanding,
my entire will—
all I have and call my own.
You have given all to me.
To you, Lord, I return it.
Everything is yours; do with it what you will.
Give me only your love and your grace.
That is enough for me. Amen.[40]

11

"Be Not Afraid"

In 1978, the world was stunned by the first non-Italian pope in more than 450 years. But the opening words spoken by this new pope from Poland were just as surprising. At his installation Mass, St. John Paul II could have addressed many important topics: war, poverty, injustice, the breakdown of marriage and family, or attacks on human life. But instead, he chose to speak directly to the hearts of modern men and women and said these three unforgettable words: "Be not afraid!"

He spoke to the many fears and anxieties that we're often susceptible to, especially in a secular age. We live in a world that thinks itself very independent, self-sufficient, not needing religion or God. But when we set God to the side, we instill in ourselves a self-reliant approach to life: we think our happiness and security in life depends all on us and how we perform. We end up constantly trying to control and manage everything, leaving us like Martha, "worried and anxious about many things."

But St. John Paul II challenged us to entrust our lives entirely to God and to cast aside all fear: "Be not afraid! Open, indeed, open wide the doors to Christ!"

These heart-stirring words from the beginning of his pontificate are full of tremendous courage that can only come from a deep, abiding total trust in God. He has a confidence that pierces through our feeble worries and fears. He exhibits a trust that breaks through our petty desires to plan and control everything. He has a faith that reminds us that we must truly seek first Jesus Christ and his Kingdom, or we will end up being slaves to the anxieties that plague our modern, self-reliant world (see Matthew 6:25–34).

To fully appreciate these words, I want you to think of an area of your life right now that you have not allowed Jesus to enter—something you've not entrusted completely to God. Maybe it is something you are worried about right now, a concern that weighs you down. Perhaps it's a hurt from your past or some situation in the present that you are exhaustingly trying control. Maybe it's a part of your life where you are afraid to let Jesus in because he might challenge you to change something or give up something. Whatever that is, imagine St. John Paul II knowing all that is inside you, knowing all your fears and worries, and then looking you in the eye and speaking the following words to you to today:

> Do not be afraid to welcome Christ and accept his power. ... Do not be afraid. Open wide the doors for Christ. To his saving power open the boundaries. ... Do not be afraid. Christ knows "what is in man." He alone knows it.

> So often today man does not know what is within him, in the depths of his mind and heart. So often he is uncertain about the meaning of his life on this earth. He is assailed by doubt, a doubt which turns into despair. We ask you therefore, we beg you with humility and trust, let Christ speak to man. He alone has words of life, yes, of eternal life.[41]

These famous words from John Paul II's inaugural papal Mass can be applied to our lives in whatever might be troubling us today. He challenges us to open wide the doors to Christ—to trust him, to not be afraid to let him fully in.

But what if we are too afraid to surrender a certain part of our lives to Christ? How do we grow in trust?

How Do I Grow in Trust?

There are five key truths to remember if we want to grow in trust.

First is *"the law of self-giving"*: When we give ourselves away in love, we actually gain so much more in return. As Jesus taught, "He who loses his life for my sake will find it" (Matthew 10:39). This is the mystery of self-giving love. In other transactions in life, if I give something away, like a twenty-dollar bill, to a friend, I lose something and my friend gains something. My friend has twenty dollars more in his pocket, while I have twenty dollars less. That's how most exchanges in life work. But that's not how love works. When I give myself away in love to God and to others, I don't lose anything. My heart actually expands and my life is enriched.

In fact, I only find fulfillment in life when I give up my freedom to do whatever I want for myself and instead use my life, out of love, to serve God's purposes. Yes, God gave us free will, but he gave it to us for the sake of love so that we could freely choose to give it away in love. And that is the most beautiful thing we can do with our freedom: give it back to God as a gift, out of love for him, and entrust our lives to his plan, allowing him to guide our lives. St. John Paul II called this mystery of freedom and love "the law of self-giving."[42]

God Doesn't Take Everything Away

Second, *God doesn't take everything away*. If we put everything in the Father's hands—all our hopes, plans, desires, and dreams—that doesn't mean he will take it all from us. Jesus calls us to put God first in life. He says we must "seek first the Kingdom" (Matthew 6:33). But when we entrust everything to him, it's not as if God plans to crush all we look forward to in life. He often just wants us to foster detachment in our hearts. He wants us to be detached and not cling to our own plans so that we can be truly open to what he wants to do in our lives.

The Father's hands are trustworthy, more trustworthy than our own. But when we willfully cling to our own dreams, our hands are not open to welcome what he wants to give us. That's why cultivating the attitude of detachment in our hearts is itself such a great blessing. We can live from a serene confidence that no matter what happens in life—whether we get what we want or not—God is always faithful and will give us what we need. The Father longs for us to trust him, to trust that, even if he allows us to experience a certain disappointment, trial, or suffering, he can bring a greater good out of it for ourselves and others.

This is the attitude Mother Teresa had. Whenever things didn't work out the way she hoped, she saw it as an opportunity to trust more in God's plans than her own: "I rejoice when something does not go as I wish—because I see that He wants our trust."[43] The Father rejoices when he sees us have a heart like Mother Teresa's, a heart of total trust and surrender.

But it's the devil who wants to steal our peace, putting fear in our heart and getting us to think that God is not trustworthy, that if we surrender to the Lord, our life is somehow going to be ruined (see Genesis 3:4–5; CCC 397). Indeed, Jesus recognizes how much we are swayed by those temptations, how little we tend to trust the Father, how we tend to cry out in worry, "What shall we eat? What shall we drink? What shall we wear? What will happen at work? What will people think? What will happen in this relationship? What about my family?" To all these anxieties, Jesus gives the same response: "Your heavenly Father knows that you need them all" (Matthew 6:32). Indeed, if we truly seek first the kingdom, God will take care of us, and give us what we need. That's what he promised: "Seek first his kingdom and his righteousness and all these things shall be yours as well" (Matthew 6:33). Like his predecessor St.

John Paul II, Pope Benedict XVI emphasized this same point in his own opening words when he was installed as Pope:

> Are we not perhaps all afraid in some way? If we let Christ enter fully into our lives, if we open ourselves totally to him, are we not afraid that He might take something away from us? Are we not perhaps afraid to give up something significant, something unique, something that makes life so beautiful? ... No! If we let Christ into our lives, we lose nothing, nothing, absolutely nothing of what makes life free, beautiful and great. No! Only in this friendship are the doors of life opened wide. ... Do not be afraid of Christ! He takes nothing away, and he gives you everything. When we give ourselves to him, we receive a hundredfold in return. Yes, open, open wide the doors to Christ—and you will find true life.[44]

God Is Faithful

Third, *whatever we don't surrender to the Lord will cause us unnecessary stress and worry.* Whatever we insist on managing and controlling by ourselves will be a constant, underlying source of agitation and unease. We will not be at rest. God wants to give you his peace. So surrender your life to him—surrender it *all* to him. Listen to the experience of the saints. They surrendered. They gave God everything and testify to the joy and happiness they found in doing so. St. Thérèse of Lisieux said, "Ah, if one only knew what one gains when renouncing all things."[45] Only when we surrender everything to God's hands will we find peace. Whatever we insist on managing on our own will weigh us down with tension and worry.

Fourth, *what displeases God most is when we don't trust him.* During their forty-year journey in the wilderness, the Israelites constantly doubted, panicked, and grumbled, failing to trust that God would protect them, provide food or drink for them, and guide them to the Promised Land. Yet God was always faithful, providing for their every need and leading them on their way, and it grieved him that his people didn't trust him.

Indeed, St. Thérèse once wrote that what displeases God most is our lack of trust. Along these lines, consider the following words God once spoke to St. Catherine of Siena, challenging us to trust in him more:

> Why do you not put your trust in me your Creator? Because your trust is in yourselves. Am I not faithful and loyal to you? Of course I am. You experience it continually. ... [All human beings] were redeemed and restored to grace through the blood of my only-begotten Son. He proved it. But it seems they do not believe that I am powerful enough to help them, or strong enough to aid and defend them against their enemies, or wise enough to enlighten their understanding, or merciful enough to want to give them what is necessary for their salvation, or beautiful enough to give them beauty, or that I have food to feed them or garments to clothe them.[46]

We can hear these words as if they were spoken to us directly. We must constantly fight against our worries, doubts, or anxieties. Those are not from God. God is good, faithful, and trustworthy. If only we remember this basic truth and allow it to penetrate the core of our being, it would go a long way to helping us overcome our fears and put our trust in him.

Fifth, *bring God's Word into whatever may be causing you distress.* This is a small but very important step in practicing greater trust in God. Say a short prayer every time you notice yourself giving in to worry. You can simply say, for example, "Jesus, I trust in you." Or you can quote a line from Scripture like Psalm 23, "The LORD is my shepherd. I shall not want." Or Romans 8:28: "In all things, God works for good in those who love him."

Arming ourselves with God's word can help us push back against the enemy and our many unhealthy fears. Bringing God's Word or Jesus' holy name into your worries is a good first step to overcoming your lack of trust in God. It reminds you of God's presence. It brings the power of his name and his Word into your troubles. It's a way for you to fight against your lack of trust.

These small acts of trust can bear much fruit over time. Even if you still feel the worry or anxiety, the act of your will to state what you *want* to live out (for example, "Jesus, I trust in you") is itself a gift to the Lord. You might not have it in you at present to free yourself from a certain worry; you might not feel like you fully trust in Jesus at a certain moment. But when you simply say, "Jesus I trust in you," you are taking an important step in your battle against those fears. By uttering a short prayer each time and quoting God's Word in those trying moments, you are fighting against the devil who wants you to lose your peace.

Mary and the Violin

Much of the work God wants to do in our souls is about learning to let go of our will, surrendering to God's plan and allowing God to act deeply in our lives—to allow him to guide all of our decisions and shape all of our actions. This deep surrender does not happen overnight; it is a lifelong process of growing in trust, allowing ourselves to be led by him and being gradually transformed.

Nor is this surrender simply about forcing oneself to do God's will; it's more about allowing God to use our lives to carry out his will through us. Mary is the model of surrender. At the Annunciation, she doesn't just submit to God's will. ("Okay, God, I accept this. If you want me to be the mother of the Messiah, I'll go along with that.") No, the Scriptures indicate that Mary *actively embraces* God's will. Her words "May it be done to me according to your word" (Luke 1:38 NAB) describe not a merely passive acceptance of God's will—like an obedient soldier carrying out his general's orders. The words point to a deeper, joyful longing to fulfill God's will. It is as if she sees what is in God's heart and, like a lover, yearns to run after her Beloved's desire. Indeed, her surrender is driven by love. Mary does not want to use her life for her own aims. She gives her freedom back to God and allows God to use her life for *his* purposes. So there's a big difference between merely submitting to God's will and allowing God to work through you like Mary did.

The Belgian spiritual writer Wilfrid Stinissen, OCD, uses an analogy about playing the violin to make this point. He describes the difference between an amateur playing all the correct notes on a violin and giving that same violin to a concert violinist to play. The concert violinist might be playing those same notes on the same instrument, but he does so with all the beauty, style, and perfection that come from his expertise. In the analogy, our lives are like the violin, and we do not want to keep the violin in our own amateur hands, clinging to our own will. Rather, we should want to hand our lives over to God who is the perfect violinist to play his most beautiful song through us.

> Before, it was I who played the violin. It was God, of course, who gave me the score, and I obediently played what he gave me to play. Now I give the violin to God and let him play. One hears that it is the same violin. It has the same characteristics and defects. But there is no similarity between the music I produced myself and what resonates now. God not only makes use of all the violin's possibilities, but he reveals something of himself in his playing. It is not that I have become more skilled. No, now the artist of the very highest grade is playing.[47]

Do you want your life to be caught up ever more into God's plan? Do you long for God to truly work through you at the deepest levels of your life—to make a beautiful song out of your life? Then learn to seek his will and truly surrender everything to his plan. God told St. Catherine of Siena that it is only to the degree that we place our confidence in him that we will experience his providence guiding our lives in amazing ways:

> This is the sign that people's trust is in me rather than in themselves: that they have no slavish fear. Those who trust in themselves are afraid of their own shadow; they expect both heaven and earth to let them down. This fear and perverted trust in their scant wisdom makes them so wretchedly concerned about acquiring and holding on to temporal things, that they seem to toss the spiritual behind their backs. ... They forget ... that I am the one who provides for everything that may be needed for soul or body. In the measure that you put your trust in me, in that measure will my providence be meted out to you.[48]

* * * * * *

What is a moment in your life when God was actively faithful to you? Thank him for the ways he provided for you in that time. Then rest in this memory with him in your prayer, letting it testify to you the truth of who he really is—good, faithful, and trustworthy.

12

Discernment: "I Don't Feel Called"?

It's something many Christians—especially young adults—seem to say in recent years: "God put it on my heart to be a leader." "I feel God is calling me to end this relationship." "I feel God is calling me to have a bigger platform." "I don't feel called to go on this retreat." "I don't feel called to continue with this group."

Taking time to discern God's will is certainly important. But I sometimes wonder how much of this "I feel called ... I don't feel called" talk really has to do with a divine call and how much it masks one's own desires and fears, likes and dislikes. In other words, how much does "I feel called" simply mean "This is what I want, and I'm going to pursue it no matter what"? And how much does "I don't feel called" simply mean "I really don't want to"?

For example, if someone from my parish invites me to be a part of a certain ministry that does not attract me, instead of honestly saying, "No thank you, I'm not interested in that," I spiritualize my no by saying, "I don't feel called." Or if I am afraid of moving to a new city for a job or for an opportunity to serve the Church, instead of saying, "I don't want to move to a place where I don't know anyone," I say, "I don't feel called." Some young people even over-spiritualize the way they end dating relationships. Instead of honestly saying, "I don't want to date you anymore" or "I don't think this relationship is working," a young man might say to his girlfriend, "I don't feel called to date you anymore," "I'm not called to be in a relationship right now," or "I think God is calling me to discern the priesthood." Indeed, some people seem so afraid of owning their decisions or admitting their preferences that they say "I don't feel called" in order to blame the Lord for the choices they make.

Why do we sometimes do this? First, "I don't feel called" can serve as a handy spiritual trump card to protect myself from truly being open to God's will. If I'm afraid of a certain possibility, I rule it out from the beginning by saying "I don't feel called." Or if I don't want to give a rational explanation for my decisions, I can just tell people, "I don't feel called." Or if I want to back out of a commitment but feel a little guilty about not fulfilling my responsibilities and letting others down, I bring God into the mix and say, "I don't feel called to do this anymore. I feel God is calling me in a different direction now." It's as if I'm saying, "It's not my fault I'm letting you down. God is the one to blame."

Trust Your Feelings?

Second, sometimes discernment can focus too much on one's feelings. Some people's rationale for their decisions might go something like this: "This is my passion, this is my dream, so this, of course, must be what God wants for me." "This makes me so excited. It makes me come alive, so it has to be God's will."

But notice how much focus there is on self in this kind of talk (*my passion*, what makes *me* excited, what makes *me* come alive). While being aware of one's feelings and desires may be a part of the discernment process, we must also remember that we are fallen human beings and not every desire or passion is from God. We often have misplaced desires, unhealthy attachments, and certain hopes and passions that are not from God. Some dreams and desires distract us from giving our best to our vocation. Others might even be sinful. Moreover, even when our desires are not bad in themselves, God often invites us to give up our preferences for good things, die to self, and do things we may not feel like doing—even things we may initially dread. Indeed, there are many things in life we are called to do that have nothing to do with how we feel.

For example, just the other night, my wife was ill and needed rest, but our toddler got out of her bed several times and came wandering in our room at two in the morning, sorrowfully saying, "Diaper. Need new diaper." My wife was the first to notice, while I remained in a deep slumber. She gently tapped me on the shoulder and asked, "Could you take care of her?" Imagine if I just rolled over and said, "No, honey. I don't feel called."

Getting out of bed at in the middle of the night to change a dirty diaper does not make me come alive. But my feelings should not be the primary part of my decision-making at that moment. In that situation, I need to rise above my feelings, because getting up to change the diaper is part of my responsibility to serve my wife and family. Similarly, God often asks us to die to our preferences and even do very hard things.

"But I Don't Feel Peace"

Third, when discerning God's will, we often seek an immediate, superficial peace instead of the deeper, lasting peace of God. It is true that we should have a certain peace about our decisions. But this does not mean God will never call us to do something that is initially very troubling. Just consider the great heroes of the Bible. Moses felt overwhelmed by God's call for him to confront Pharaoh and lead the people out of Egypt. The prophet Jeremiah was worried that he was too young for the daunting task of calling people to repentance. Even the Blessed Virgin Mary "was greatly troubled" when God called her to become the mother of the Messiah (Luke 1:29). Imagine if these heroes said no to God's call simply because they felt great trepidation. It's hard to imagine Mary telling the angel Gabriel, "No, thank you. I am greatly troubled by this call. I don't feel peace."

God often called the great saints out of their comfort zones to do things that were very difficult, scary, and painful. We've seen how Mother Teresa experienced inner turmoil about being called to leave her beloved Loretto Sisters, start a new order, live radical poverty, and endure the possibility that she might fail in this endeavor. But underneath those initial, superficial fears, one detects in Mother Teresa a deeper, more important fear: *a fear of not doing what God wants for her,* a fear of letting her fears and self-interest control her and prevent her from pursuing God's will.

Jesus does not offer the kind of superficial peace the world offers. He says, "Peace I leave with you; my peace I give to you; *not as the world gives do I give to you*" (John 14:27, emphasis added). The world's peace is based on comfort, ease, enjoyment, and self-interest. Worldly peace is based on getting what you want and thinking that will make you secure. But Jesus wants to give us a much deeper, lasting peace. It's true the Bible teaches that the Lord "will give you the desires of your heart" (Psalm 37:4), but it's not your superficial desires for attention, praise, success, pleasure, or comfort that he wants to fulfill. It's the *deepest* desires on your heart which are for him and his plan. And sometimes his plan is not what we expect. Sometimes it goes against what we had in mind. Sometimes it's hard, difficult, uncomfortable, and very demanding. Sometimes it calls us to give up our own plans, die to ourselves, and be stretched like never before. It always involves the Cross.

Think of Jesus' own example in the garden of Gethsemane. As he faces the immediate prospects of all that is about to happen to him, he agonizes in prayer, sweating drops of blood. The idea of being betrayed, beaten, scourged, and crucified was utterly horrifying. That kind of suffering is repugnant to human nature. So if Jesus is truly human, it's no wonder he prays, "My Father, if it be possible, let this chalice pass" (Matthew 26:39). He looks at death square in the eye and acknowledges how hard his Passion is going to be. But since Jesus is also divine and his human will is perfectly united to the divine will, he does not allow himself to be a slave to those emotions. He immediately embraces the Cross that is coming to him and prays to the Father, "Not as I will, but as you will" (Matthew 26:39).

In Dialogue with God

St. Ignatius of Loyola taught that we should not make a decision based on our initial emotional response to a new possibility. Often, those first feelings of fear or anxiety are not a sign of God's will but an indication of a disordered attachment we have. We are too attached to a certain plan for ourselves, a certain relationship, a certain comfort, a certain way of life. So when God's will presents itself to us, we respond in fear and dread. God's peace is a deep, abiding peace in our souls, and is not usually found in our superficial, initial responses to God's will.

When discerning God's will for our lives, we should have the disposition of Mary at the Annunciation. Though she was "greatly troubled" by the angel's initial message, she remained open to God's will. Indeed, Mary rises above her initial fearful feelings. She does not allow herself to be a slave to her emotions and desires. She remains in dialogue with God, talking to him about what he is asking of her.

Many of us, however, when we're afraid of some new direction or possibility, don't remain in dialogue with God. Out of fear, we cut off the conversation as quick as possible. We immediately tell ourselves, "Oh, that's not a big deal. I'm fine. I don't need to change. I don't have time. I could never do that. No, God doesn't want me to give that up!" Some Christians don't even sincerely talk to God about what he wants because they are so afraid that God's will won't match up with their own!

How about you? When you sense God might be calling you to do something or inviting you to give up something, how do you respond? Do you ask the Lord what he might be asking of you? Do you talk to him about it? The next time you sense the Lord might be inviting you to make a change in your life, make a sacrifice, tell someone sorry, give up something, or go in a different direction, talk to God about it: "Jesus, are you asking me to do this? Is this your will for me? Is this the right thing to do?" Tell him you are troubled. Tell him why you are afraid of this new possibility. Ask him for the grace to do his will, even if it is very difficult. What do you have to lose by talking to God? You have everything to lose if you *don't* talk to him about it in prayer.

* * * * * *

In your prayer, call to mind an area of your life where you've been reluctant to ask God what he thinks about something. Ask yourself why you have been afraid to talk about this with the Lord. Then enter into a dialogue with him about this area of your life, listening attentively for his perspective and invitation.

Part Four

INTERIOR PEACE

13

Your Unexpected Crosses

It's easy to meet God in the good spiritual activities we plan, like taking time for prayer or reading a good Christian book. But it's harder to meet him in the difficult things we *don't* plan—the inconveniences, disappointments, fears, and sufferings that regularly come up in life: A car breaks down. A kid breaks down. A friend lets us down. How do we respond when those unexpected crosses show up on our doorstep?

Don't think the spiritual life is only about what happens between you and God in the chapel. God wants to meet us in those unplanned circumstances just as much as he wants to meet us in our prayer time. Indeed, those unexpected crosses are often the places God invites us to grow most.

There was a man in the Bible who faced an unexpected cross—quite literally—and his life was changed forever. His name was Simon of Cyrene. You might be familiar with him from the Fifth Station of the Cross. Simon helped Jesus carry his cross on Good Friday, and devotional books have long celebrated him as a model of Christian service, someone who inspires us to have more compassion and help people carry their burdens.

But I've always wondered about this classic take on Simon of Cyrene. I remember as a seventh grader thinking, "That doesn't make sense! How is Simon a model of service? He didn't volunteer to help Jesus that day. He didn't do it out of compassion. He did it out of compulsion!" After all, it's not as if Simon woke up on Good Friday and said to himself, "Oh, it's Friday—that's prison ministry day. I'd better go out and find a prisoner to help today." No. He was just one of the many Jewish pilgrims coming into Jerusalem for the Passover feast when Roman soldiers suddenly forced him to carry Jesus' cross to the place of execution. What an interruption to Simon's day!

But Luke's Gospel subtly shows us that Simon was changed through his encounter with this unexpected cross. Luke gives one little detail that points to how Simon had a conversion: Simon took Jesus' cross and carried it "behind" Jesus.

That little detail is telling. For earlier in Luke's Gospel, Jesus himself said, "If any man would come after me, let him deny himself and take up his cross daily and follow me" (Luke 9:23). So according to this verse, what is the standard of discipleship? Taking up a cross and following Jesus. What is Simon doing? Taking up a cross and following Jesus, all the way to Calvary.

With these little connections, Luke's Gospel is subtly showing us what many in the early Church knew: that Simon of Cyrene was transformed through his encounter with the unexpected cross and became a Christian. Notice how Simon didn't plan this cross as part of his goals for his spiritual life. Nor did he run away from it when it suddenly arrived. It was not his will, not his preference. It was forced upon him. And yet, by surrendering himself to the situation and choosing to accept what he did not wish for himself, he found, in the end, much more than pain and sorrow. He also found the Love for which he was made. He found his salvation.

What God did for Simon through the unplanned cross is what he wants to do for us: meet us in the unexpected trials that come up in life so that we can discover how God is inviting us to become more like him.

Don't Run Away

In every cross, there is always some treasure, some important spiritual lesson, some hidden grace that God wants to give us. So when we experience trials in life—loneliness, a financial stress, a problem a work, a broken relationship, a health issue, a challenge in marriage—we shouldn't just see the hardship. We should also look for the spiritual gem, the invitation to grow in some way, that God has in store for us inside that cross. That's why, when these trials come our way, we should always pray, "Lord, what are you trying to teach me? What are you trying to show me? How are you inviting me through this challenging circumstance to change or grow or love more?"

When troubles come, the temptation is to just look at our problems and be crushed by them, either getting discouraged or finding ourselves anxiously scrambling to solve them. But God wants to teach us something in every moment, even in our troubles. So the next time you experience a challenge in life, take a moment to look inside your soul. Ask God what he is wanting to point out to you through this trial and how he might be inviting you to grow. Don't miss the moment of grace.

Indeed, the events that God allows to unfold in our lives are some of the most powerful spiritual teachers he gives us. We must remember this important truth: if, in God's providence, he permitted something to happen, he can use it for our good. "In everything God works for good with those who love him" (Romans 8:28). Sometimes, he uses difficult circumstances to help us learn to depend more on him and less on ourselves. Other times, he can use crosses to put his finger on something he wants us to notice about ourselves, to get us to look deeper into our heart to discover the roots of our many sins, weaknesses, and insecurities: Why did I respond that way? Why am I frustrated? What am I really afraid of? Why do I feel hurt?

Still other times, God allows us to experience a cross because he is inviting us to grow in a new way: Maybe God is allowing me to experience some setbacks and obstacles so that I grow in patience. Or perhaps God is allowing me to experience some suffering so that I grow in compassion for others who suffer more than I do. Maybe God permits me to make a mistake or even fail so that I grow in humility. Or maybe he's leaving me in darkness without understanding where my life is going so that I grow in trust and learn to walk more by faith and not by sight. Growing in any of these things—patience, compassion, humility, and childlike trust—would be good for my soul. And sometimes it takes difficult circumstances to get us to grow in these virtues in a more significant way than we could on our own. So whatever happens in life, we must remember that God is in charge and if he permits something to happen, he can use it for good. Indeed, no matter what events unfold in the external circumstances of our lives, we should always have the confidence that God can bring some important good out of it on the inside for our soul.

To sum up, think of the crosses that come up in life as places to encounter Jesus. They're almost like "mini-tabernacles." We are used to bending our knees before the Real Presence of Jesus in the Sacred Hosts kept in the tabernacles of our churches. But, in an analogous way, do we bend the knees of our hearts before the trials that come our way? Do we seek to encounter God in those moments? For Jesus wants to meet us in those difficult situations that he has, in his providence, allowed us to experience. He wants to meet us in the crosses in life, not just in the chapel.

* * * * * *

Ask God to bring to mind a trial or challenge in your life right now. Then ask him, "Lord, how are you trying to meet me in this unexpected cross? What are you trying to teach me? How are you inviting me to grow and change?"

14

The Present Moment

*"We can indeed say that we do not have our past
troubles or those which are in the future; all we have
is the moment of time in which we are now."*[49]
– St. Catherine of Siena

Do you tend to worry about the future? Or do you tend to play your mistakes over and over again in your head? One thing that keeps us from giving the best of ourselves to God in prayer is failing to live in the present moment.

God is not waiting for us in some imaginary future that may or may not happen. Nor is he seeking us in a regrettable past event that has already been completed. He's here for us in the present. Part of what God wants to do in our prayer life is to cultivate a heart that is present to him throughout the entire day, that seeks his will and serves him right now in the present moment. As Jesus taught, "Let the day's own trouble be sufficient for the day" (Matthew 6:34).

The Past

We can be weighed down by things we've done in the past, whether a long time ago or something that took place recently. We can churn over in our minds some failure, mistake, or embarrassing moment.

Maybe it's something we said. A decision we made. The way we treated someone. A failure in parenting. A ball we dropped at work. We wish we could take it back. We worry about the implications. We wonder what others think of us now. "I'm so foolish. Why did I do that?" Maybe there's some sin we committed, and we can't let it go. We feel great shame and continually condemn ourselves for it.

These regrets about the past can crush us. They keep us from giving our attention to how God wants to meet us in the present. The only thing we can do is to surrender those past regrets into God's hands. If we've apologized to the people we hurt, if we bring our sin to Confession, if we've done what we can to set things right and make up for any wrong we've done, then there's nothing more we can do.

But you still worry or feel burdened by your past action? Then that's precisely where God wants to meet you right now, and he's inviting you to grow in the virtue of hope. He wants you to surrender it to him, trusting that he can bring some good out of your mistakes. He really can write straight with your crooked lines. Maybe God allowed you to make a certain mistake so that you would avoid worse ones in the future. Or maybe he allowed you to fail at something because you struggle with perfectionism and he wants you to find your identity in him, not your performance. Perhaps the hurt you inflicted on someone motivated you to take a closer look at how you treat the people around you and strive to relate to them better. Maybe your fall into a certain sin has led you to a profound encounter with God's mercy. Indeed, some of the worst sinners become some of the greatest saints; those who are forgiven much love much (see Luke 7:47).

God really can bring good in us from our faults and failures. That is what our Faith tells us. Do you really believe this? The past event is done and has been dealt with. It's your lack of trust that God wants to work on now. Accept the reality of what you've done. Don't carry out a court case in your head about your mistake.

Surrender it to him. Trust that he can bring some good out of it and stop letting it fill your mind. Move on so that you can give all your thought, attention, and energy to God, the people in your life, and whatever you need to be doing right now.

Fears for the Future

Another thing that keeps us from encountering God in the present is worry over the future. We can play the "what if" game and unnecessarily stress ourselves over things that may or may not happen: what if a health issue gets worse, a financial situation doesn't improve, a relationship doesn't work out, or the company doesn't give you the promotion you want? We can spend a lot of time worrying about imaginary sufferings that might or might not come to be. But the anticipation of suffering is not reality. The suffering doesn't exist yet. Yet the worry over a suffering that might unfold in the future is sometimes more difficult to endure than the suffering itself if it comes to pass. A Christian disciple should not be weighed down by imaginary crosses in the future: "Let the day's own trouble be sufficient for the day" (Matthew 6:34).

God wants us, of course, to give due attention to our responsibilities in life and think about the steps we need to take to plan for the future. That's part of the virtue of prudence. God wants us to think through in advance our projects at work, make good decisions for our children's education, and plan ahead for our family's finances. But we should never be anxious about these things. Anxiety is not from God. Jesus says, "Do not be anxious" (Matthew 6:34). There's a big difference between prudent concern and unnecessary worry or anxiety. Any time we notice we are losing peace about something, becoming anxious about something, it's like the check-engine light in our car going off. It's a sign that something is seriously wrong. Something significant is not functioning well in our spiritual life.

If a certain concern is consuming us, distracting us from what's most important in life, that's a problem. St. Thomas Aquinas even teaches that our anxiousness can be sinful when we give a concern too much weight—when we have much fear that will lack what were need or we think we absolutely must have this particular thing in order to be happy ("I have to have this work out the way I want. Unless I get this job / keep this relationship / get this opportunity, my life is ruined. I fear I will never be happy unless this happens.")

Most of our fears turn out to be imaginary. Things usually are not as bad as we at first dreaded. But we should always trust that, even if our worst fears should turn out to be true, God can still bring good out of it—good for other people, good for the Church, good for the world, and even good for me. If there's something burdening you now, some worry about the future, surrender that worry to the Lord. Name that fear. Talk to Jesus about it. But also tell him you don't want to be afraid. Ask him to help you trust him more with this worry. Even if you can't control your emotion of fear, you can still make an act of the will—right now—and tell the Lord, "Jesus, I want to trust in you. I don't want to be a slave to this fear. Help me trust in you." Tell him that. Tell him that, even if this suffering you can foresee unfolding should indeed occur, you want to trust in his Providence—you want to trust that he will help you through that cross, that he will take care of you and can bring some good out of it for your life.

Whenever I fall into the trap of worrying about the future, my wife often reminds me of this. She never lets me play what she calls the "what if" game. She often says, "If that scenario ends up happening, we can worry about it at that time. God will give us the grace to deal with it then, when we need it. But it hasn't happened yet, so we don't have the grace to deal with it now. It's simply not worth spending too much time thinking about it at this moment."

The twentieth-century Jewish writer Etty Hillesum makes a similar point. And her words come from the horrific experience of living under Nazi rule—first being thrown into a Jewish ghetto in the Netherlands and then carried off to Auschwitz, where she was killed. Though she had no control of her destiny and was living in the day-to-day uncertainty of what might happen next, she wrote about her complete confidence in God and the importance of maintaining peace. Any fears about what may or may not happen in the future need to be immediately brushed away like fleas:

> We have to fight them daily, like fleas, those many small worries about the morrow, for they sap our energies. We make mental provision for the days to come, and everything turns out differently, quite differently. Sufficient unto the day. The things that have to be done must be done, and for the rest we must not allow ourselves to become infested with thousands of petty fears and worries, so many motions of no confidence in God. Everything will turn out all right. ... Ultimately, we have just one moral duty: to reclaim large areas of peace in ourselves, more and more peace, and to reflect it towards others. And the more peace there is in us, the more peace there will also be in our troubled world.[50]

* * * * * *

Ask the Holy Spirit to reveal something in your past or something you worry about in the future that you have been too focused on. As it comes, simply pray, "Jesus, I trust in you," surrendering that thing to him and returning to the present moment with him.

Part Five

THE FIRST STEP UP IS DOWN

15

Weakness

There's a certain weakness you've been struggling with for a long time, a sin you keep bringing to Confession. You want to change, try hard to change, and beg the Lord to help you change. Why doesn't God seem to be helping you?

God is all-good and all-loving—doesn't he desire your holiness and perfection? He's also all-powerful. Certainly, he has the *ability* to remove your faults. So why doesn't he come down and equip you to conquer all your sins right now?

These are questions faithful Christians are likely to ask at some point in their walk with the Lord. When we run up against the heavy weight of our own weakness, we must first ask ourselves if we are really trying hard enough. Perhaps we need to make a more radical break with sin, put in more effort, exercise more self-control, or have more resolve to practice virtue and eradicate our faults. As Mother Mary Francis reminds us, the art of following Jesus as a disciple demands a lot of us. Just as achieving excellence in a certain skill or profession requires much discipline, practice, and determination, so does the art of being faithful to Jesus:

Sometimes a little child will say, "It's so hard to be good!" And so we have to practice. It is hard to become a concert pianist. It is hard to become an expert surgeon. It is hard to become an outstanding ballerina. We have to practice and practice and practice. If this is true of the worldly arts, it is more true of the art of spiritual fidelity. Sometimes in our slothfulness or our fear we are doing the equivalent of saying to God, "It's so hard!" I think God says to us, "You don't practice enough."[51]

But there may be another reason for our ongoing struggles that has nothing to do with us finding some inner strength to pull ourselves together and defeat our worst sins. God once told St. Catherine of Siena that sometimes he leaves certain souls in their weaknesses—on purpose, as part of his plan! "Sometimes my providence leaves my great servants a pricking, as I did to my gentle Apostle Paul, my chosen vessel. After he had received my Truth's teaching in the depths of me the eternal Father, I still left him the pricking and resistance of his flesh" (see 2 Corinthians 12:7).

In this dialogue, God refers to a battle against sin which the Apostle Paul faced in his own life. Think about Paul's amazing accomplishments. Before his conversion to Christianity, he was already an incredibly gifted individual, a student of one of the most eminent Jewish teachers of his day, a leading Pharisee, and under the Jewish law, utterly blameless (Philippians 3:4–7). He then had a direct encounter with Jesus Christ on the road to Damascus and became a Christian. After years of intense prayer and study, he became one of the most powerful Christian evangelists the world has ever known, successfully spreading the Gospel throughout Asia Minor, Greece, and Rome. He stands out as one of the most important leaders in the early Church. On top of all that, he also had a profound interior life, receiving many visions and revelations of the Lord and even being caught up spiritually into heavenly paradise (2 Corinthians 12:1–4).

And yet alongside these extraordinary accomplishments, virtues, and spiritual experiences, he still had a habitual struggle with a particular sin, a "thorn in the flesh" which he could not overcome no matter how hard he tried. Why this constant ordeal? Paul explains that God allowed him to struggle with this thorn to keep him humble—to "keep me from being too elated by the abundance of revelations" he received (2 Corinthians 12:7). St. Paul begged God to free him from this persistent temptation, but God said to him, "My grace is sufficient for you, for my power is made perfect in weakness" (2 Corinthians 12:9).

We Learn Compassion

God in no way intends for us to sin. And he always gives us the grace we need: "My grace is sufficient for you." But sometimes, in his wise and gentle Providence, he allows people to keep struggling with certain weaknesses. God has the ability to remove the thorn himself, but he chooses not to at the present moment. And he does this for a reason: for our good. We should trust that God can use even our struggles, defects, and sins to bring about some good in us. He's so powerful he can even use our sins as opportunities for us to grow our spiritual lives.

According to St. Catherine, one reason God might allow a thorn in the flesh to persist is to help a person grow in love of neighbor and become more compassionate when he encounters other people's faults. The more he realizes how weak he is, the more patient he will be with the people around him. Instead of being surprised or frustrated with their shortcomings, he gradually will become more gentle and understanding, sympathizing with others instead of judging them. As God explained to Catherine, "For those who suffer themselves are far more compassionate to the suffering than are those who have not suffered."[52]

We Learn the Truth about Ourselves (Humility)

A second reason God might leave a thorn in those he loves is "to keep them in the self-knowledge whence they draw true humility."[53]

Nothing teaches us humility more than a profound experience with the reality of our own weakness. This is much more than saying, "I am a sinner. I have many weaknesses. I need God." It's easy to get the right answer about humility on a catechism test: Are you wounded by Original Sin? Yes. Do you have a lot of faults? Yes. Do you need God in your life? Yes. That's what we can call an *intellectual* humility.

But God wants to bring us to something deeper, something that can be called *experiential* humility. He wants us to experience, at the core of our being, the honest truth about our ourselves—how impoverished we really are and how much we really depend on God.

When people, for example, become more in touch with the real shortcomings in their marriage, in their parenting, in their abilities at work, in the way they respond to certain situations, in the way they treat other people and in their relationship with God—when they start to realize that perhaps they have been overestimating their virtues, that they don't have it as much together as they thought—this dose of reality cannot help but awaken a bit of humility.

Similarly, when people start to notice how much they fall into gossip, worry about what others think of them, judge others and compare themselves to others—when they become aware of how attached they are to their own interests, plans, and comfort; how much their hearts are tainted by selfishness, pride, and lust; or how much their souls are full of fears, anxieties, and troubles—they cannot help but be humbled. They might be highly successful in their careers, well liked in their communities, and very involved in their parishes. They might go to daily Mass, listen to Catholic podcasts, and participate in faith formation groups. Yet when they run up against trials they cannot avoid and weaknesses they cannot change, they are forced to realize how little control they have over their lives. They come to terms with how weak they really are and how much they really need the Lord. As God explained to St. Catherine, "You cannot arrive at virtue except through knowing yourself and knowing me. And this knowledge is more perfectly gained in time of temptation, because then you know that you are nothing since you have no power to relieve yourself of the sufferings and troubles you would like to escape."[54]

Consider another medieval saint's description of this kind of true humility. The twelfth-century saint Bernard of Clairvaux emphasizes how important it is for a person to really know himself. This is not about a quick glance at your soul and giving the nod: "Yes, I have some imperfections. I guess I could use God's help a bit." Rather, true self-knowledge entails a hard, honest look inside, not making any excuses, any rationalization, any downplaying of the faults we see. St. Bernard says, "There must be no dissimulation, no attempt at self-deception, but a facing up to one's real self without flinching and turning aside." He then goes on to allude to St. Paul's "thorns" of weaknesses that constantly "prick" us. Here's how St. Bernard depicts a man who lives from a place of true self-knowledge:

> How can he escape being genuinely humbled on acquiring this true self-knowledge, on seeing the burden of sin that he carries, the oppressive weight of his mortal body, the complexity of earthly cares, the corrupting influence of sensual desires; on seeing his blindness, his worldliness, his weakness, his embroilment in repeated errors; on seeing himself exposed to a thousand dangers, trembling amid a thousand fears, confused by a thousand difficulties, defenseless before a thousand suspicions, worried by a thousand needs; one to whom vice is welcome, virtue repugnant? Can this man afford the haughty eyes, the

proud lift of the head? With the thorns of misery pricking him, will he not rather be changed for the better? Let him be changed and weep, changed to mourning and sighing, changed to acceptance of the Lord, to whom in his lowliness he will say: "Heal me because I have sinned against you."[55]

Notice what self-knowledge, according to St. Bernard, entails: a profound awareness of the utter fragility of the human condition. This is not just "Yeah, I have some faults. I struggle with sin. I need God's grace to help me." This is a person convinced of his feebleness, keenly aware of how little he is in control of his own life and how utterly dependent he is on God—for everything.

And if we're honest, isn't this our experience in life? Are we not all weighed down by various burdens and concerns of this world? Are we not all easily swayed by countless temptations and sinful inclinations? Are we not all affected by a thousand fears, worries, suspicions, and difficulties? The man who dares to look inside himself and see all that is there cannot help but cry out to God for help. He realizes, not just intellectually but in his deep experience of himself, how weak he is and how much he needs God. And that self-knowledge, that profound realization of how things really are—that humility—is crucial if we want to go deeper in relationship with God.

* * * * * *

What is one area in your life where you've been rationalizing a certain fault or making excuses for your weaknesses? Invite Jesus to be with you in that place and talk to him about how much you need him.

16

"Drunk with Love"

"You must be drunk with love!"

That was St. Catherine of Siena's response to the overwhelming love of God. From a human perspective, it seems incomprehensible that God would love us—we who are so weak, sinful, forgetful, ungrateful, unfaithful. What would God see in souls like us? He must be drunk if he loves us this much!

Catherine's amazement over divine love points to a third reason God might permit us to struggle with a certain weakness or sin: to know and experience God's love personally at a deeper level.

We saw in the last reflection how God can use our struggles with sin to help us grow in compassion for our neighbor who also has many shortcomings. We also saw how God can use our weaknesses to help us grow in humility, in greater awareness of how much we need God. Indeed, growing in love and patience for neighbor and growing in true self-knowledge are two very good things for the soul. But there is a third reason God may allow us to struggle with sin: to give us the opportunity to experience his love for us in a whole new way. We might know in our heads the basic Christian message, "God loves you!" But do we know it deeply in our hearts? Have we experienced God's love as the saints have, in a way that turns our world upside down and transforms our entire outlook on life?

The fundamental fact of God's unconditional, merciful love takes on an entirely new meaning when we face the truth about ourselves—our brokenness, our darkest sins, our deepest wounds, our greatest fears. Only when we come to terms with how selfish, proud, controlling, sinful, fearful, and untrusting we can be, will we fully appreciate God's amazing love for us. It's as if God says to us, "I know all you have done. I know all you are struggling with. I know how weak and imperfect you are. I know your sin. *And I love you even here. You are beloved in my sight.*"

That's the encounter God wants us to have with him. He wants us to experience this most unexpected love. When we face the truth of our many failures and find in God not disappointment, wrath, and scorn but love and mercy waiting for us there, we discover a love much of the world does not know. It is a love not based on my performance—not based on how many good Catholic things I do, how well I keep the commandments, and how often I avoid falling into sin. Rather, we encounter an authentic love that cannot be earned. It is a love so lavishly and freely given we might think that there's been some mistake, that the teacher graded the wrong paper, that we need to do something to make ourselves worthy of such a gift first. And yet that gets to the very heart of the matter: there's absolutely nothing we can do to earn this love. We can't earn love from our parents. We can't earn it from a coach. We can't earn it from a boss or from a friend. And we certainly cannot earn it from God. Love cannot be earned. It can only be received, and God freely gives his love. "But God shows his love for us in that while we were yet sinners Christ died for us" (Romans 5:8).

That's the lesson St. Catherine came to understand in her own life, and she marveled over this most unexpected love of God, even calling him a "mad lover": "O mad lover! And you have need of your creature? It seems to me, for you act as if you could not live without her. She runs away from you and you go looking for her. She strays and you draw closer to her.'"[56]

The Gentle Mirror

Coming to terms with our weaknesses leads to a greater knowledge of God. And this brings us to a most important point: Do you look at your many faults and weaknesses the way God wants you to look at them? Or do you view them the way the devil wants you to? God wants you to see your faults the way he sees them—through what St. Catherine calls "the gentle mirror" of his love.[57] But the devil wants you to look down at your wretchedness and never look up at God's mercy.

The devil will use even our genuine sorrow over sin to keep us staring at our mistakes and get us to lose hope. Catherine explains that the devil, "under the guise of contrition and hatred for sin and sorrow for her guilt," tries to lead the soul into a preoccupation with self—with his own failures—in such a way that fosters self-condemnation and despair. "I'm horrible. I'm such a mess. I hate that I do that." In other words, the devil wants to keep us focused on ourselves and not on God. He wants to keep us beaten down and frustrated with our repeated failures instead of turning to God's mercy—because he knows if we discover the amazing love and mercy of God, our hearts will be so captivated by the Lord that we will never want to turn away from him again.

This is why we must zealously resist these temptations of the enemy. We must fight against the temptation to stare at our faults and failures alone, and instead see our sins in light of the merciful eyes of the Father and our relationship with him. St. Bernard of Clairvaux makes a similar point: "As long as I look at myself, my eye is filled with bitterness. But if I look up and fix my eyes on the aid of the divine mercy, this happy vision of God soon tempers the bitter vision of myself. ... In this way ... self-knowledge will be a step to the knowledge of God."[58]

Indeed, the more I know the truth about myself and all my poverty, the more I learn the truth about God—how kind and merciful he is, ready to forgive, ready to help and heal us. Only when we dare to meet God there in the valley of our faults can we come to a deeper appreciation of the truth about the God who is love and the profound truth about ourselves which St. John Paul II explains: "We are not the sum of our weaknesses and failures; we are the sum of the Father's love for us and our real capacity to become the image of his Son."[59]

Learning to meet God there—in our weakness, in true humility—is the key, we will see, to our deepest transformation.

* * * * * *

Ask God to reveal to you a place in your life that you have been prone to contemplating your own sinfulness apart from him. Then, in humility, in the full truth of your many shortcomings and sins, turn your gaze toward God and pray, "Father, show me how much you love me!"

17

The Valley of Humility

My little kids love to color pictures for me to hang up in the office. Sometimes I'll come home from work, and they rush to the door to show me their works of art from the day. "Daddy, this is for *you!*"

The three-year-old's pictures are usually just a bunch of scribbles. I'll hold up her indecipherable, scribbled drawing and ask her, "So what did you draw for me, sweetie?" And she might reply, "That's *you,* daddy!"

What would you think if, at that moment, I tore up the paper and said, "This is a terrible drawing! Don't you ever draw a picture for me again until you get it exactly right!" No good father would do that. As a father, I'm moved by the fact that my children are thinking of me and wanting to give me a present. I see a lot more than a bunch of scribbles. I see their love and their desire to give me a gift.

There may be areas of our lives where we feel like we've only drawn a bunch of scribbles: My marriage has a lot of tension. My prayer life is all over the place. The way I parented one of my children—if I had the chance to do it over again, I would do things so differently. There's something I did a long time ago that I wish I could take back. There's some weakness I'm struggling with right now that's so embarrassing. Where is my life going? Just a bunch of scribbles.

God the Father, however, sees in us so much more than the scribbles we have drawn with our lives. No matter what we've done, no matter how many times we've failed, he sees our heart today—he sees the regrets we might have, the sincere sorrow over our sins, our desire to be better. To have a repentant and contrite heart is a very good thing. That means we are not rotten to the core—we are *not* just a bunch of scribbles. There is a noble part of us that feels bad about our failings and sincerely wants to live more like Christ. God sees that goodness in our heart and delights in it. Like the Father in the parable of the Prodigal Son, God runs to meet us when he sees that slightest movement of goodness in our souls. In the words of St. John Paul II, "The father sees so clearly the good which has been achieved" in the repentant son "that he seems to forget all the evil which the son had committed."[60] When he sees a truly contrite heart, the Father not only overlooks our scribbles; he delights in us and seeks to heal our brokenness, bring some good out of our mistakes, and write straight with our crooked lines—if we dare to meet him in the valley of humility.

The Impossible Summit

St. Thérèse of Lisieux once shared important advice about what to do when we feel overwhelmed by our weaknesses.

We might look at our many shortcomings and get discouraged. We might feel like we have a tall mountain to climb in order to overcome our faults and grow in holiness. It's as if God is on top of the mountain of holiness waiting for us, but we are so weak and small and unsure if we will ever be able to make our way up to him.

St. Thérèse, however, would be concerned that we are traveling on the wrong road, that we have a misguided notion of the quickest path to God. She offered some beautiful advice to a sister who was feeling overwhelmed by the immense gap between God's holiness and her own many imperfections. Thérèse said to her, "I see clearly that you are mistaking the road. ... You want to climb the mountain, whereas God wishes you to descend it. He is awaiting you in the fruitful valley of humility."[61]

What a beautiful image! God waiting for us not on top of the mountain of sanctity, but down low, where we are, in the valley of humility.

Indeed, God wants to meet you—the real you—where you are, right now with all your faults and all your scribbles. You may not have made a masterpiece out of your life, but it's the real you, as you are, that God wants to meet.

He doesn't want to meet the ideal "you" that you hope to become someday. He doesn't want to meet the well-put-together "you" that you like to present to your friends, family, and colleagues or the carefully crafted "you" that you project on social media. He wants to meet the *real* you, with all your sins, wounds, fears, and failings. He wants to meet the you that is weighed down by anxiety, that wants to control everything, that worries too much about what other people think, that can't handle imperfection in yourself or in others, that has real struggles in your family life. He wants to meet the "you" that struggles in prayer and so often falls into sin. That's the real you, where you are today.

And even if you have areas of your life that you think are just a bunch of scribbles, the Father still delights in you and wants to transform you. He wants you to receive his love, forgiveness, and healing power. He wants to turn those random scribbles into a beautiful masterpiece.

But the first step is to meet God *with* your failures, not in spite of them. God is not waiting for you on top of some imaginary, perfect mountain of holiness—*because that's not where you are*. You are down low in the valley. And he longs to meet you there, because that's where *you* are, as you are, with all the messiness in your life. Will you dare to be vulnerable with God, to surrender to the fact of your hurts and weaknesses and allow him to encounter you there? It's only when you dare to let God to meet you as you really are, with all your sins and scribbles, that he can help you, carry you up the mountain, to the heights of his love—heights to which you could never ascend on your own.

* * * * * *

How does St. Thérèse's image of meeting God in the valley and not the summit change the way you think about the path to holiness? Prayerfully consider some of the "scribbles" you have in your life. Show God those scribbles. In prayer, tell him about them and allow him to meet you as you are, with all those imperfections.

18

Three Battles in the Valley

We saw in the last reflection how God wants to meet us as we really are, with all our defects, failures, and sins, in the valley of humility. Three things, however, keep us from meeting God in this way: self-justification, self-reliance, and self-condemnation. These are, in the end, different forms of pride, which is a refusal to accept the truth about oneself.

First, *self-justification*. We don't want to change, give up something, or admit we are wrong. So we make excuses for ourselves: "I was tired." "It was just this one time." "I wasn't feeling well." Or we blame other people: "He started it." "My boss doesn't understand." "It's her fault. She made me respond this way." Or we rationalize our sins. We try to convince ourselves that what we're doing is okay, that we don't need to change: "It's not a big deal." "Everybody else watches this show." "I'm not hurting anyone." "I'm not as bad as other people." "It's just a few times." "God doesn't mind." But when pridefully we can't even admit we have a certain weakness or sin, we will never be disposed to all the graces God wants to give us to heal us of our many imperfections.

Second, *self-reliance*. We might be tempted to think that all we need to overcome our sins is more will-power, more commitment, more self-control. We adopt a Nike approach to spirituality. How do we become a saint? "Just Do It." That, however, is not the Gospel message. The whole point is that we *can't* just do it. As fallen creatures, we are fundamentally broken and need God's help. We might pridefully wish that we were perfect and did not need to depend on God's mercy and grace as much as we do. But growing in holiness is all about growing in our dependence on God. God is inviting us to rely more on him and not on ourselves.

Third, *self-condemnation.* We can be so frustrated with ourselves when we sin: "I hate it when I do that! Why am I like this? Why can't I change?" Those voices in our heads, however, are not from God. They are from the devil. Scripture calls the devil "the accuser" (Revelation 12:10). He wants to accuse us and beat us down with shame and self-condemnation so that we don't look up and discover the truth of how gentle, patient, and merciful God really is. So if you have those self-condemning thoughts, rebuke them. That's not what the gentle and merciful voice of God sounds like.

And don't try to tell yourself it is humble to beat yourself up like that. This kind of self-reproach is not humility. It may, in fact, be a form of spiritual pride. Notice how we're not so much concerned about our relationship with God when we do this. We're more focused on ourselves. All the pronouns are first person singular: "*I* hate it when *I* do that! Why can't *I* change?"

Imagine a husband who hurt his wife. Imagine if instead of looking his wife in the eye to apologize and express his heart-felt sorrow over having hurt her, he went to a corner to mope about his mistakes. "Why am I such a bad husband? I hate when I do things like that! I really need to be better and stop making these same mistakes." How would that self-centered remorse make the wife feel? The husband is focused on himself, not her. He's more upset over his failures—over the fact that he is not living up to his self-imposed standards for himself—than he is concerned about his wife and their relationship!

The same is true when we hurt our relationship with God. When we fall into self-condemnation, it might be a form of spiritual pride. We're not so worried about repairing our friendship with God. We're more distraught over the fact that a certain view we have of ourselves has been shattered: "I can't believe *I* did that. *I* should be so much better!" As Fr. Jacque Philippe explains,

> The sadness and the discouragement that we feel regarding our failures and our faults are rarely pure, they are not very often the simple pain of having offended God. They are in good part mixed with pride. We are not sad and discouraged so much because God was offended, but because the ideal image that we have of ourselves has been brutally shaken. Our pain is very often that of wounded pride! This excessive pain is actually a sign we have put our trust in ourselves—in our own strength and not in God.[62]

As we grow in prayer, God invites us to be more vulnerable with him. He wants us to come to him as we are, with all our scribbles, in the valley of humility. There in the valley is where Jesus does his amazing work of healing and transforming us. That's why the devil will do all he can to keep us from going there. So let us stop pretending, posing, and projecting an image of ourselves to the world, to our friends, to God, and to ourselves. Let us never fall into the devil's traps of self-justification, self-reliance, or self-condemnation. Let us instead dare to face the truth about ourselves and, with St. Thérèse, meet God in the fertile valley of humility.

* * * * * *

Which of these three forms of pride do you recognize most in your own life—self-justification, self-reliance, or self-condemnation? Ask Jesus to forgive you for this pride. Then, in your own words, express to him your love for him, your trust in him, and your conviction that he alone has the power to save you.

19

A Little Way

Her faults did not displease God.

That's the important lesson St. Thérèse learned on a retreat in 1891—an insight that would shape the rest of her life. For years she had struggled with discouragement over her many defects. But on this retreat, a Franciscan priest gave her words of encouragement that launched her "full sail upon the waves of confidence and love" from which she would never look back: "He told me that my failings did not displease the good God." This priest also assured her that God "is well satisfied with [her] soul."[63]

This was good news for the young Thérèse. She personally felt overwhelmed by the gulf between the perfect holiness of God and her own many inadequacies. Though she aspired to be holy, she was acutely aware of her imperfections. As she later reflected, "I have always wanted to be a saint. Alas! I have always noticed that when I compared myself to the saints, there is between them and me the same difference that exists between a mountain whose summit is lost in the clouds and the obscure grain of sand trampled underfoot by the passers-by."[64]

But now, she would not let herself get discouraged. She would not let the weight of her imperfections keep her from pursuing a path to holiness. She knew that if God had given her the desire for holiness, the desire to love him completely with all her heart, there must be some way to reach it, even if ascending the mountain seemed impossible. So she set out to find another way, "a little way, a way that is very straight, very short, and totally new."[65]

In the late nineteenth-century world of St. Thérèse, the elevator was a new technological innovation. And it gave her a picture in her mind for what she was seeking spiritually: an elevator that could carry her to God. "We are living now in an age of inventions," she wrote, "and we no longer have to take the trouble of climbing stairs, for, in the homes of the rich, an elevator has replaced these very successfully. I wanted to find an elevator which would raise me to Jesus, for I am too small to climb the rough stairway of perfection."[66]

St. Thérèse's Two Bible Verses

Thérèse searched the Scriptures for some sign of a spiritual elevator, some way for her to be lifted to God. Two passages stood out to her.

The first was Proverbs 9:4: "Whoever is a little one, let him come to me."[67] What moved Thérèse to delight in this verse was the fact that God was *inviting* those who are spiritually small, poor, and weak to come to him. Notice how the small and weak are not rejected by the Lord. God does not say in this verse, "Whoever is a little one, get out of my sight! Get your act together and grow up spiritually! Don't you dare come near me until you root out all your weaknesses!" Nor are they merely permitted to be in his presence, as if God begrudgingly allows it: "Whoever is a little one, well, I guess you can be here. I'll let you in." No. The weak and the small are *summoned* to draw close to God! It is as if they are the honored guests! So even with our many imperfections, if we remain small and humble, we are bidden by Our Lord to draw near. Our defects don't displease him.

A second verse that stood out for Thérèse was Isaiah 66:12–13: "As one whom a mother caresses, so I will comfort you; you shall be carried at the breasts, and upon the knees they shall fondle you."[68]

From this verse, she saw that even if she approaches God humbly, like a child, as she really is, in the valley of humility, God would carry her as a mother carries her helpless little one. Jesus would carry her up the mountain.

She rejoiced in the fact that her littleness did not have to be an obstacle to holiness. Indeed, it could be a pathway to holiness if she dared to entrust herself to the merciful arms of God. For by meeting God in her weakness, coming to him small and helpless like a child, she had the confidence that Jesus would lift her up the mountain of sanctity faster and higher than she could ever get on her own. Jesus would be the spiritual elevator she was looking for: "Ah! never did words more tender and more melodious come to give joy to my soul. The elevator which must raise me to heaven is Your arms, O Jesus! And for this I had no need to grow up, but rather I had to remain *little* and become this more and more."[69]

Holiness, Not Perfectionism

But what does it mean to remain little? Does this imply some kind of passivity in her spiritual life, just kicking back, relaxing, and waiting for the elevator to take her to holiness? Certainly not. St. Thérèse taught the importance of sincere effort, striving to give our very best to God. She, in fact, did everything she could to try to root out even the slightest of her weaknesses and pursue holiness at each moment. But her Little Way also taught that, in the end, real sanctity is not about perfectionism: never making mistakes, never falling, never needing God's mercy, never having to depend on God. That's not Christianity. The Gospel message is about learning to entrust our faults to God's mercy and rely on his grace more and more for everything in our lives. A true disciple always lives from a place of this fundamental truth Jesus taught: "Apart from me, you can do nothing" (John 15:5). The more we learn to depend on God, the more our little good works and feeble attempts at virtue become imbued with his infinite love.[70]

So rather than getting distraught over our many scribbles and shortcomings or overwhelmed by the arduous ascent to some self-imposed summit of sanctity, we are encouraged by Thérèse to line up among the imperfect in the valley of humility, trusting that God sees our good will and our desire to rely completely on him. In a letter to her sister Celine, she explains that if we remain small, humble, and utterly convinced of our total dependence on God, the Lord will do amazing things in our soul. But if we think we can get far up the mountain on our own, if we are not truly convinced at the core of our being how much we really need God's help for everything, then God will leave us to attempt the impossible ascent on our own: "So let us line up humbly among the imperfect," she wrote, "let us esteem ourselves as *little souls* whom God must sustain at each moment. When He sees we are very much convinced of our nothingness, He extends His hand to us. If we still wish to attempt something *great* even under the pretext of zeal, Good Jesus leaves us all alone."[71]

In my family, I have one little child who wants to be very independent. She prefers, for example, to put on clothes and shoes all by herself and often resists getting help from others. If someone tries to assist her, she grabs the article of clothing and cries out, "Do it self! Do it self!" So even if we know she's going to have a hard time getting her shoes on or buttoning her dress by herself, we sometimes leave her to her own devices to learn the hard way that she needs to depend on others. She can't always "do it self!"

At the same time, if I happen to hear the same child suddenly tumbling down the stairs, the thud of her body hitting the floor and a scream, "Help!" I drop everything to rush to her, comfort her, and make sure she's okay. And after she calms down, I help her up the stairs so she can arrive at her destination safely and quickly in my arms.

When God sees that we have not surrendered ourselves to him, that we're not truly relying on him—that we're still trying to control everything, plan our lives on our own, and not depend on him—then God honors our freedom and leaves us on our own. But when we stumble, fall, and realize how much we need his help, how much he must sustain us at every moment—when we *surrender* to the truth of how little we can do on our own and how very much we really do depend on God for everything—then our heavenly Father will always rush to our assistance and carry us.

Practically, how do you live this out? How do you surrender to the truth of your littleness? Of course, you must always try, give your best effort, do all you can to overcome sin, practice virtue, deny yourself daily, and take up your cross and follow Jesus. Like a little child, you must try to "raise your little foot to scale the stairway of holiness."[72] But even if you will not get very far or be able to prevent yourself from falling, you can still surrender to the truth of your weakness—you can accept the fact that you so very much need God's help. And you can trust that God sees your good will—he sees your heart and your sincere desire to love him, not just your falls, your sins, your scribbles. And you can have total confidence that the Father will be so moved by your humble dependence on him that he will meet you at the bottom of the stairway to help you up.

* * * * * *

Imagine yourself as a little child in the valley of humility, one of the "little ones" from Proverbs 9:4. As a child, speak to your Father about one of your greatest weaknesses, your littleness, and express to him your need for his help.

20

Attracting Grace

One of St. Thérèse's sisters, Marie, felt a bit overwhelmed by the saint's exceptional devotion to the Lord. After Thérèse shared with Marie her passionate desires to give herself completely to God—to be a Carmelite, a spouse, a mother, an apostle, a warrior, a missionary, a Doctor of the Church, a martyr, and even offer herself as a victim of love to God—Marie came away a bit dejected. She didn't feel that she was as holy as Thérèse because she did not notice those same burning desires in her own heart:

> Like the [rich] young man in the Gospel, a certain feeling of sadness came over me in view of your extraordinary desires for martyrdom. That is the proof of your love; yes, you possess love, but I myself! no, never will you make me believe that I can attain this desired goal, for I dread all that you love. This is a proof that I do not love Jesus as you do.[73]

At this, Thérèse quickly wrote back telling Marie that she has missed the whole point of her Little Way. What pleases God in Thérèse is not her bold desires but her accepting, indeed, loving her weakness. It's precisely because she recognizes the truth of her feeble condition that she can love so much:

> Dear Sister, how can you say after this that my desires are the sign of my love? ... Ah! I really feel that it is not this at all

that pleases God in my little soul; what pleases Him is that
He sees me loving my littleness and my poverty, the blind
hope that I have in his mercy. ... That is my only treasure. ...
Why would this treasure not be yours?[74]

Let's ponder that line: *"What pleases him is that he sees me loving
my littleness."* We saw how, earlier in her life, Thérèse learned from
the Franciscan priest that her defects do not displease God. Now
she articulates a clear understanding of what positively *does* please
the Lord. What pleases God the most is not grandiose desires and
heroic self-willed attempts to scale the mountain of sanctity. What
pleases God most is our humility. He delights when we express
how much we need him. He rejoices when we see ourselves as
we really are—weak, fragile, and completely dependent on him—
and surrendering ourselves to that reality, abandoning our entire
lives to his care. What a beautiful truth this is: we don't have to
fix all our problems and scale the mountain of perfection before
daring to meet God. If we are humble, we can meet him right now
in the valley and be lifted up the mountain by him. Indeed, when
we come to him with such humility and trust, it is as if he cannot
resist picking us up in his arms, holding us, and carrying us to new
heights in the spiritual life that we could never attain on our own.

St. Bernard of Clairvaux, in a remarkable statement, describes
how this kind of humility actually "attracts grace." We don't just
passively receive grace. We can *attract* it! And we do so most
powerfully not through setting out to conquer some spiritual goal
on our own, but by facing the honest truth about our many faults
and imperfections—that we are not as patient, kind, generous, or
devoted as we might think and certainly not as much as we ought.

Indeed, when we put ourselves in the presence of the all-holy
God, we cannot help but face the truth of our own unholiness. And
that humble recognition attracts God's grace more than anything
else. It "puts an end to haughtiness of the eyes, attracts grace and

prepares for the leapings of the Bridegroom. ... I have learned nothing is so efficacious for the gaining, the retention and the recovery of grace as to discover that in God's presence you must always stand in awe rather than yield to pride."[75]

The Heart of the Little Way

So what does this look like? Practically, what do I need to do to be "loving my littleness" and living out what Thérèse called her "Little Way"?

Just a few months before St. Thérèse died, her sister Pauline asked her to sum up this Little Way. Thérèse answered: "It is the way of spiritual childhood, the way of *trust* and *absolute surrender*."[76] From this we can see the two pillars of her Little Way: surrender and trust.

St. Thérèse knew that most of us don't exhibit the heroic virtue and extraordinary sanctity found in the stories of the great saints. But all of us, right now, with all our inadequacies, can follow Thérèse in her *Little Way* of holiness. All of us—even the weakest among us—can learn to surrender and trust more. That's within our reach. We might not be able overnight to conquer all our sins, acquire all virtue, and reach the highest levels of mystical prayer. But we can all, right now, no matter how many defects we have, grow in *surrender* and *trust*. Let's consider these two key words Thérèse herself used to sum up her Little Way:

- *To surrender:* We cannot change our past actions. And we might not at present be able to change the fact that we have a certain fault. But the one thing we can do is accept it. We can accept it as a fact, accept our poverty, accept the truth of our many defects, accept the truth of our complete dependence on God, and surrender it all to the Lord.

- *To trust:* We cannot change what we have done, and we may not have it in us at present to overcome a certain weakness.

But we can place all our confidence in Jesus, trusting in his mercy and trusting that the Lord will forgive us and heal and transform us in his time and in his way.

And we can do this right now. In prayer, we can express to the Lord our surrender and trust: "Jesus, I struggle with X. I have done Y. I have hurt the people I love in these ways. I have hurt my relationship with you. I am sorry. I will sincerely try my best to change, but first, I accept that this is who I am right now. I *surrender* these weaknesses to you. And I *trust* that you can forgive me in your rich mercy and that you can heal me of this weakness with your grace."

You don't need to be a superstar saint to do this. Anyone, even the weakest and littlest of souls, can learn to surrender to God this way. All we have to do is meet God in the valley of humility and trust that he will carry us up the mountain. Remember, it is not our imperfections that offend God. As Thérèse explains, "What offends Jesus, what wounds his heart, is lack of trust."[77]

So the primary issue is not whether I had an impure thought, lost my temper, spoke an unkind word, or didn't pray today. We are all going to make mistakes and fall. The more fundamental issue is about what I do when I fall. Do I overlook how my lack of faithfulness hurts my friendship with God and others? Do I rationalize and make excuses for my faults? God cannot help me if I choose to be mediocre.

Or do I get discouraged, frustrated, and beat myself up over my failings? God cannot help me when I am so self-centered. Let's not be so surprised and self-occupied with our imperfections. If we truly know ourselves, we know how little we can do on our own. Falling should not be so shocking. Thérèse, instead, invites us to throw ourselves into the Father's arms like a child, trusting in the Father's love.

Indeed, when one of my children does something wrong but right away realizes it, feels bad about it, and comes to me with a kiss saying, "I'm sorry, Daddy," my heart melts. When they come into my arms with humility, love, and confidence in my love for them, I can't help but forgive them. I can't resist. The same is true with our heavenly Father.

In a practical expression of the Little Way, the spiritual writer Mother Mary Francis put it this way: "Be faithful when you're not faithful." When you stumble, at least be faithful in admitting you were unfaithful. At every fall, at every moment of unfaithfulness to God, we have the opportunity to be faithful by responding with a contrite heart, repentance, a determination to be better, and most of all, complete trust in the Father's love and mercy. "This is the heroism: not that we never fall, but that we keep on rising. ... We can be very faithful in our contrition. We can be very faithful in our humility. We can be very faithful in admitting that we were wrong. We can be very faithful in saying, 'I could have done much better.' ... When we are so wholeheartedly contrite, God tells us, 'I don't even remember what happened.'"[78]

Litany of Trust

In conclusion, to pull together the themes we've been discussing in the last several reflections—the themes of humility, surrender, and total confidence in the Lord—let us reflect on the following beautiful prayer, known as "The Litany of Trust," by the Sisters of Life:

From the belief that I have to earn Your love,
     Deliver me, Jesus.
From the fear that I am unlovable,
     Deliver me, Jesus.
From the false security that I have what it takes,
     Deliver me, Jesus.
From the fear that trusting You will leave me more destitute,
     Deliver me, Jesus.

From all suspicion of Your words and promises,
> Deliver me, Jesus.

From the rebellion against childlike dependency on You,
> Deliver me, Jesus.

From refusals and reluctances in accepting Your will,
> Deliver me, Jesus.

From anxiety about the future,
> Deliver me, Jesus.

From resentment or excessive preoccupation with the past,
> Deliver me, Jesus.

From restless self-seeking in the present moment,
> Deliver me, Jesus.

From disbelief in Your love and presence,
> Deliver me, Jesus.

From the fear of being asked to give more than I have,
> Deliver me, Jesus.

From the belief that my life has no meaning or worth,
> Deliver me, Jesus.

From the fear of what love demands,
> Deliver me, Jesus.

From discouragement,
> Deliver me, Jesus.

That You are continually holding me, sustaining me, loving me,
> Jesus, I trust in you.

That Your love goes deeper than my sins and failings, and transforms me,
> Jesus, I trust in you.

That not knowing what tomorrow brings is an invitation to lean on You,
> Jesus, I trust in you.

That You are with me in my suffering,
> Jesus, I trust in you.

*That my suffering, united to Your own, will bear fruit in this life
and the next,*
> Jesus, I trust in you.

*That You will not leave me orphan, that You are present in
Your Church,*
> Jesus, I trust in you.

That Your plan is better than anything else,
> Jesus, I trust in you.

*That You always hear me and in Your goodness always respond
to me,*
> Jesus, I trust in you.

That You give me the grace to accept forgiveness and to forgive others,
> Jesus, I trust in you.

That You give me all the strength I need for what is asked,
> Jesus, I trust in you.

That my life is a gift,
> Jesus, I trust in you.

That You will teach me to trust You,
> Jesus, I trust in you.

That You are my Lord and my God,
> Jesus, I trust in you.

That I am Your beloved one,
> Jesus, I trust in you.[79]

* * * * * *

*Which line from the Litany of Trust challenges or
encourages you most? Why? Take time to talk with God
about that line, asking him what he's trying to teach
you through those words from the Litany of Trust.*

Part Six

HEALING
THE
SOUL

21

Healing the Whole Person

A woman had been hemorrhaging for twelve long years. Imagine the shame, isolation, and sorrow she must have experienced month after month, year after year.

Her condition was not debilitating or contagious, but it was socially devastating. Ever since she started hemorrhaging, the blood never stopped flowing. Nor did the embarrassment or the loneliness that ensued. She was not able to interact normally with others, for in the first-century Jewish world in which she lived, she would have been in a perpetual state of ritual impurity. Anyone who touched her would instantly be made ritually unclean themselves (see Leviticus 15:25–31; Ezekiel 36:17). So according to the customs of the time, she had to stay away from others—and this humiliating social distancing had lasted for twelve years.

She felt helpless. She had tried everything. She had spent all her living on doctors, but no one could cure her of her strange malady.

And then one day, when Jesus was passing through the streets of her town, she caught a glimmer of hope. She had heard about Jesus' many miraculous healings and hoped he could do something for her. Given her condition, however, she was afraid to ask him for help. According to the purity laws, she shouldn't even draw near him, especially with the crowds that were pressing in around him. And so, timidly, she snuck in behind him to touch just the fringe of his clothing, saying to herself, "If I only touch his garment, I shall be made well" (Matthew 9:21).

In that instant, power went forth from Jesus, and her hemorrhaging stopped. What twelve years, a lifetime of savings, and many doctors could not do, Jesus accomplished through this one simple touch. Nevertheless, *she was not yet fully cured*—and that's the most important part of this story. Her physical ailment may have ceased, but there was a deeper healing Jesus wanted to do for her.

Jesus asked the crowd, "Who was it that touched me?" (Luke 8:45). At first, the woman was frightened. She was caught! For her to touch someone else usually meant the person would become ritually unclean. Jesus knew what she had done, and she was going to have to reveal herself. She came forward trembling, fell before Jesus, and in the presence of all the people, she gave witness to how she was miraculously cured. Jesus did not respond with anger because she broke the purity laws. Instead he said, "Daughter, your faith has made you well; go in peace" (Luke 8:48).

Deeper Healing

When we read stories about Jesus' healing miracles, we might be impressed by his power over blindness, deafness, leprosy, or in this case a persistent hemorrhage. But did you know that Jesus wants his healing power to go even deeper? More important than curing some people physically of their diseases and infirmities, Jesus wants to heal all of us spiritually of our sins and weaknesses. He wants to heal us socially, restoring our ability to enter into healthy relationships with those around us. He wants to heal us emotionally of all the wounds that keep us from flourishing in life and from giving ourselves entirely to God. And this happens not just in extraordinary circumstances or only in exceptional Christians. This is the work Jesus wants to do in *all* souls, all the time. He wants to make us whole.[80]

Consider what happens at the climax of this Biblical scene. Jesus does not merely cure the woman of her hemorrhaging. By declaring in the presence of the crowds that she has been made well, Jesus *heals her socially*, liberating her from her isolation and restoring her to her community. By calling her "daughter," Jesus shows she has been *healed spiritually*. He is welcoming her into the supernatural family of his disciples, the Family of God. She is received as a daughter of God. And by telling her, "Go in peace," Jesus gives the woman a gift the world cannot give, a gift promised to those who respond to Christ's kingdom (see Luke 1:79; 2:14, 29; 7:50; 10:5-6). Because of her great faith, she is made well on all these different levels.

Indeed, Jesus' saving mission involves healing the whole person. He wants us to be able to love the Lord with all our heart, soul, strength, and mind. So every aspect of our personalities must be converted, healed, and transformed into Christ's likeness. Jesus wants to heal everyone of their sins, vices, disordered desires, unhealthy emotions, wounds from the past, false-perceptions of reality, and the lies they tell themselves—everything that keeps them from encountering God's love and being transformed by that love at every level of their lives.

This healing of our wounded human nature has often been likened to a rod of iron that is placed into fire. The heat of the fire changes the iron rod. It makes the iron start to change color, becoming orange or red like fire. It makes the rod become hot and emit smoke, like fire. Indeed, the iron itself begins to take on the characteristics of fire.

Similarly, when we allow the fire of Christ's Spirit to penetrate the depths of our soul, we are changed. Christ begins to live his life more profoundly through us, and we start to take on the character of Christ. We begin to think like him, love like him, serve like him, value what he values, and love what he loves. We become patient in areas where we used to be impatient. We forgive when we used to hold a grudge. We take initiative and volunteer to serve when we used to sit back and let others do the work. This change happens gradually, often without our even noticing. And it is not our doing. It is the Holy Spirit working through us. Jesus is changing our heart and healing us at the deepest levels so that his love can truly radiate through us. We can begin to say with St. Paul, "It is no longer I who live, but Christ who lives in me" (Galatians 2:20).

Do you want to be healed in this deep way?

Healing Our Desires

God wants his healing power to penetrate the core of our being, all the way down to our desires. That's how much God loves us. He doesn't just want our obedience. He wants our hearts. That's why God doesn't want us merely saying, doing, and believing the right things. He also wants us to want those good things.

When I first asked my wife out on a date, I didn't merely want her to say yes. I wanted her to want to go on a date with me. Imagine if she said yes only because she felt obliged to for some reason: "Well, I really don't *want* to go out with you on a date, but I feel sorry for you, and my spiritual director challenged me to make a sacrifice this week. I don't want to hurt your feelings, so I guess I'll make this sacrifice and go out with you just this one time." How disheartening that would have been!

Similarly, God doesn't want us merely to say yes to his moral law and his plan for our lives. He wants us to *want* to follow him in all that he has in store for us. He wants our hearts.

But God also knows we are fallen human beings. Because of Original Sin, we are wounded. Our desires are often in conflict with what is truly best for us. We want to be good, virtuous men and women, but our fallen desires take us in many different directions. As St. Paul admitted, "I do not do what I want, but I do the very thing I hate" (Romans 7:15). A part of us sincerely wants to live in purity, but we sometimes follow our lustful desires instead. We want to be kind and patient with others, but we notice our anger getting the best of us. We know there's an important and difficult task to be completed, but we keep procrastinating. There's a constant battle between our desire to do God's will and our fallen desires.

Self-Control

There are times when temptation is so strong and our desires are so powerful, we just need to practice self-control and say no. That ability to resist temptations to evil desires, especially when they are most vehement, is what St. Thomas Aquinas calls *continence*[81]—an important virtue to have. But it's not one we ideally want to depend on all the time. It's like using the emergency brake in the car. It's good to have the emergency brake when you need it in emergency situations. But if you find yourself in emergency situations on the road every day, there's probably a deeper problem with your car— or your driving!

Similarly, having continence—the ability to resist powerful, unhealthy desires within you—is important to have in emergency situations. But if you find yourself having to use it all the time, that's a sign of a deeper problem in your soul. Wouldn't it be better if your desires were working *for* you instead of *against* you? Wouldn't it be better if you didn't have to rely on the emergency brake all the time? Wouldn't it be better if your desires were pushing you more in the right direction, assisting you in virtue and carrying you on toward where you really want to go in life, rather than being something you have to battle against constantly?

God wants to get to the root of our sins. He wants to heal those fallen desires themselves. Growth in virtue and holiness is not primarily about having disordered desires and resisting them. It's more about God healing those errant desires and transforming them into healthy, well-ordered desires. And then, on our end, it's about giving in to those good desires that God places on our heart.

Indeed, this is the essence of the New Law that Christ offered the world. It is not a law written on tablets of stone or some lofty ethical standard that we have to desperately reach for but a law the Holy Spirit writes in our hearts (see Ezekiel 36:26–27; Jeremiah 31:33), awakening our deepest desires, prompting us to do good, and giving us the grace to do it.

As we grow in holiness, we begin to realize that God's will is not something merely outside of us. The more we learn to cooperate with God's Spirit in our hearts, shaping our desires, we begin to realize that doing God's will is not so much making a sacrifice and performing some difficult, heroic task for the sake of the Lord. Rather, we are, in the end, simply pursuing what we most deeply desire to do. As Simon Tugwell explains,

> We shall not, if we are truly motivated by charity, be able to say with some self-satisfaction, "Now I have really done something for God!" We shall still have to say that we have only done what we really wanted to do. And that gives little ground for vanity. ... Christian growth should make it harder and harder for us to identify God's will as something external to us, so we shall be less and less able to indulge in the pleasant feeling of a pampered good conscience. God is not just the policeman trying to keep us in order, or the examiner waiting to see our papers; he is also the great seducer, wooing us into his paradise of delights, so that his own joy may be in us, and our joy may be full. And this is that full human freedom, which ... [is] the condition of a man "whose heart is large from the abundance of grace, so that he does whatever he does for God, simply because he wants to."[82]

That's the goal: to be so transformed that our hearts are beating in perfect harmony with Christ's. Indeed, Jesus helps us come in touch with our truest, most noble desires—the desires he has placed in the depths of our hearts, which are for him and his plan. Over time, we may find that something we so passionately wanted to pursue, we don't seek as much anymore. Certain dreams we had for ourselves are no longer as attractive. Certain plans we desperately clung to, we begin to let go. Certain fears that enslaved us no longer hold us back. Indeed, the more we spend time with Jesus in prayer, the more our hearts are softened, and we interiorly begin to want what he wants, to seek what he seeks, to love what he loves. His desires become our desires. And this process of transforming our desires is less about giving up something and more about embracing something more. Our desires have become so shaped by Jesus that what he wants and what we want become one thing. We become like a lover who wants to be with the beloved and do what the beloved wants to do. The more we fall in love with the Lord, the more we *want* to spend time with him and do his will. Pursuing the will of our Beloved is no longer such a heavy sacrifice. We are simply doing what we most deeply desire to do.

* * * * * *

What's a place in your life where your desires need to be healed— where you seek the wrong things or even do good things more out of obligation than out of love. Invite the Holy Spirit to soften your heart and write the law more deeply on your heart so that you can live even more from the depth of your own desire.

22

Healing Our Desires

The more we grow in prayer, the more profoundly we come in touch with those deepest desires, the deepest thirsts, that God has placed in our souls—those desires that go beyond anything this world can offer, those desires which are for him and him alone. No amount of success, praise, or pleasure can satisfy. The more we are aware of those infinite longings in our hearts and cooperate with them, the less we will eventually find ourselves attracted to the things of this world, the things that hurt us, distract us, and cannot satisfy.

St. Bernard of Clairvaux once explained, "Sweetness conquers sweetness as one nail drives out another." In other words, if we want to conquer our disordered desires, our attraction to sin, our deepest vices, we can't just drive out those desires by resisting them with the emergency brake. Some bad habits, vices, and addictions run too deep for us simply to say no to them. We need a greater force pulling us, drawing us in the other direction. We need to discover a greater sweetness, the sweetness of the Lord.

My kids love ice cream. But let's say, for some strange reason, I decided that I don't want them to eat ice cream anymore. I am not likely to be successful in steering them away from their ice cream cravings by proclaiming a new family edict that says, "No! Ice cream is bad. Don't ever eat it!" Every time they see ice cream at the store they will desire it. Every time they go to a birthday party, they will have a hard time saying no when the ice cream is served.

But if I can get them to taste something that's so much better than their favorite Dairy Queen ice cream—something that will attract them so much, they won't even be interested in it anymore— then they will be able to rise above their lower, unrefined cravings and experience something that is much more satisfying. And that something is *gelato*. Gelato is not just Italian ice cream. It's an entirely different experience. It has been said that gelato is almost an eschatological sign—a foretaste of the heavenly banquet! Indeed, when I took my children to Italy and they tasted gelato for the first time, that's all they wanted. They didn't miss their store-bought ice cream. The taste of gelato far surpassed anything they could experience in the United States. And their hearts were restless until they rested in gelato.

Similarly, the healing of our sinful desires will involve much more than mere continence, the emergency brake, the will power to resist them. We must be drawn by a greater force. "Sweetness conquers sweetness as one nail drives out another." This is another reason why growing in prayer and the cultivation of the interior life is so important. Through prayer, we encounter our heart's *deepest* desire, the only thing that can satisfy: God himself. By living in greater awareness of this infinite thirst in the depths of our souls, our emotions and desires can be healed, and the Lord can lead us to what we most truly seek.

Four Stages of Growth

To more fully appreciate the amazing work God wants to do in our spiritual lives, let's take a look at four stages of development based on the writings of St. Thomas Aquinas.[83] These four general stages involve the development of virtuous emotions and desires and point to the profound healing God wants to perform in our souls.

First, let's start on the most sinful side of the spectrum: a *vicious person* has bad desires, habitually acts on those bad desires, and has no remorse. He thinks there is nothing wrong with what he is doing. A certain married man, for example, desires to have affairs with other women, acts on those desires, and rationalizes his adultery by telling himself, "Well, my wife hasn't been treating me well lately, so I need to get my emotional and sexual needs met elsewhere. It's her fault. And besides, I'm not hurting my wife. She will never know." Having evil desires, habitually acting on those desires, and not recognizing those actions as evil is the vice of intemperance.

Second, a *weak-willed person* may have disordered desires and act on those bad desires but at least realize that what he's doing is wrong. He maintains a correct judgment on what is good and what is evil and knows that correct judgment doesn't resonate with his wrong actions. Here, consider another married man who has lustful desires and acts on those desires by having an affair just as the first man did. But let's say this second man knows what he is doing was wrong and feels bad about his actions. He may even bring it to Confession and resolve to resist this sin next time. This man lacked self-control. He was weak-willed. He realized what he was doing was wrong, but he did not have enough virtue to resist doing it.

In a third stage of moral development, we have the *self-controlled person*. This is someone who has bad desires, but he knows his sinful desires are wrong, and he resists them. A married man in this case might notice in himself sexual desire for a woman who is not his wife. He would like to act on that desire and have an affair with this woman. He thinks about it a lot, but he knows adultery is wrong and does not want to act on the sinful desire. So when she eventually propositions him, he battles against those evil desires and successfully resists them. He tells her no. He uses the emergency brake and practices continence, or self-control.

And it's a very good thing that he does. But it is still far from ideal. Imagine the husband coming home from work, saying to his wife, "I thought about having an affair today. I really wanted to do it. But I was so good. I resisted that temptation and told the woman no." That's not going to go over very well! The self-controlled person resists sinful desires. The virtuous person, however, does more: he desires to do what is good from his heart.[84]

The fourth and highest stage of moral development is found in the *virtuous person*—someone who not only correctly judges what is good and evil and does what is right, but also desires rightly; he has healthy desires. He "feels the desire to do the right thing, with no conflicting desires impeding one's good actions."[85] He desires what is good and is repulsed by what is evil. The married man in this case does not simply avoid committing adultery. He does not want to have an affair. He loves his wife and desires to keep his heart entirely dedicated to her. This doesn't mean he never faces temptations of lust. But they are just that—temptations coming from outside of him, not desires in his heart that he has sought out or intentionally cultivated. Whatever sensual reaction might spontaneously start stirring within him, he does not allow himself to give in to it. He looks away, says a prayer, and rises above those unprompted thoughts and reactions within him. He desires to be pure of heart and undivided in his love for his wife.

It's important to notice that what makes the virtuous person virtuous is not merely the absence of sinful actions or unhealthy desires. It's the presence of virtuous emotions and well-ordered desires. But in many areas of our lives, those can only be formed through prayer and cooperation with the healing power of God's grace.

A New Heart, A New Spirit

Most faithful Christians probably find themselves living between stages two and three, between falling into sin because we are weak-willed and avoiding sin by exercising self-control. We know we shouldn't lose our temper, we try not to lose our temper, and sometimes we're successful. But in certain circumstances, we give in to our angry desires—we say an unkind word to our spouse, we raise our voice with the children, we get overly frustrated in a meeting—and we feel bad about it. Similarly, we know we shouldn't spend so much time on our phones and on social media, and sometimes we are disciplined about our screen time. But the gravitational pull toward our phones is still there and we find ourselves turning to them over and over again. Most of us tend to oscillate between having moments of practicing good self-control and moments of being weak-willed, not able to resist our unhealthy desires.

Few of us, however, would describe ourselves as living at the fourth and highest level of virtue. Our desires themselves still need to be healed. Though we can begin to experience the freedom and growth God has in store for us right now, getting to the highest level of transformation often takes a lifetime—and even into purgatory. The roots of our disordered desires run deep.

That's why God didn't just give his people a law—a list of rules to follow. With all our unhealthy desires, we could never fulfill the law on our own. We need God's help. We need his grace. As St. Augustine once said, "The law was therefore given, in order that grace might be sought; grace was given, in order that the law might be fulfilled."[86] But let's seek God's grace not only to help us overcome our sins. Let's beg him to heal the *roots* of our sins: our disordered desires and attachments. Let's beg him to give us a new heart and a new Spirit. That is what he promised to do (Ezekiel 36:26–27; Jeremiah 31:33). He promised to send his Spirit and write his law in our hearts, healing our desires and prompting us to walk in his ways. We can only be made whole if we allow God to heal us like this from within.

* * * * * *

Which of the four stages in the formation of desire do you most identify with—vicious, weak-willed, self-controlled, or virtuous? Ask the Holy Spirit to help you imagine what it will be like to be in the fourth stage of moral development, where your desire for the good is strong and steadfast. Ask the Holy Spirit to help form you into that person. And ask him to show you one concrete step you can take this week that moves you more in that direction.

23

Healing Our Wounds

God wants to draw very close to us. But there can be times when his presence might feel *uncomfortably* close—when he calls us, for example, to repent, give up something, or trust him more or when he is rooting out sin and attachments that need to be removed. As good as the process of healing our desires can be for us, it can also be hard and scary.

But his closeness can be particularly painful when he touches parts of our lives that we might rather forget. Jesus wants to enter every aspect of our being and fill it with his love. That includes hurts from our past that continue to affect us in the present. These wounds, if not treated, can fester, become infected, and cause deep, long-term problems in our souls—in our ability to love and receive love, to trust others, to enter deep friendships, to build a strong marriage, to build a strong family life, and most of all, to live our relationship with God.

Some of us were not welcomed when we entered this world. Maybe our father was not involved in our life or our mother didn't have time for us when we were young. Some of us come from dysfunctional families with a lot of anger, anxiety, manipulation, pressure to succeed, or pressure to act in certain ways. The wounds inflicted in these situations are real, and they may affect the way you live for many years. Jesus wants to fill those wounds with his love.

Some of us were ill-treated at school. Some of us were abused or experienced other kinds of trauma. These aren't just mere facts about our lives like "I'm Catholic. I have blonde hair and blue eyes. I'm married with three children, and I am an adult child of divorce." These wounds shape us. They affect our relationships. They influence how we handle conflict, stress, and pressure. They shape our view of ourselves and others. Most of all, they affect how we view God. As Mother Teresa explains, "The hurts of life and sometimes our own mistakes—[may] make you feel it is impossible that Jesus really loves you, is really clinging to you."[87]

So if you start to notice that you're a little more sensitive than others in certain areas, that you have certain insecurities, anxieties, unhealthy emotional responses, a need to impress, a fear of conflict, a desire to control every detail, a desire to be esteemed by people on screens who don't really know you, an over-achiever side that's compensating for a lack of unconditional love in your life—this may be God making you aware of something that is broken in you, putting his finger on something that he wants to heal.

Suffering With

The mystery of Good Friday reminds us that every wound we have experienced, God has experienced first. God does not remain separate from us. He has compassion in the truest sense of the word—the Latin root word for compassion means "suffering with." He entered into our suffering. God became man in Jesus Christ and, from the very beginning of his life, experienced rejection, humiliation, and poverty. There was no room for him in the inn. The God of the universe was born among the animals and placed in a manger.

Throughout his public ministry he was unwelcomed, misunderstood, criticized, unappreciated, taken for granted, used, forgotten, hated, opposed, and plotted against. In his Passion, he was betrayed, abandoned, rejected, unjustly condemned, beaten, abused, and murdered. As Pope Benedict explains, "Man is worth so much to God that he himself became man in order to *suffer with man in an utterly real way—in flesh and blood*—as is revealed to us in the account of Jesus' Passion. Hence in all human suffering we are joined by one who experiences and carries that suffering with us; hence *con-solatio* is present in all suffering, the consolation of God's compassionate love."[88]

So no matter what we have experienced, we can never say to God, "You don't understand me. No one understands me. No one has any idea what I have gone through." He's already been through it. "He has already suffered everything," writes Wilfrid Stinissen. "All fear, loneliness, and disappointment have been gathered together in him. It has received a positive stamp by the fact that he has gone through it. Every time a painful memory comes back, you can, so to speak, welcome it in Jesus' name. All your memories are also his memories, and your wounds are his wounds."[89]

And that's a crucial point to grasp. It's not just that you have your sufferings and Jesus has his sufferings. It's more than that. Because he lives in you, your sufferings become his sufferings. Jesus already has descended into the depths of whatever pain you have experienced. He is waiting to meet you there with his love. He is present to you in your wound and invites you to join your life to his, right there, in your cross, so that he can raise you up, lift you from the mire and make you new. There, in the valley of darkness, Christ's light can still shine, and you can be healed, your suffering can be redeemed, and God can bring some good even out of the evil you experienced.

The Lord Is with Us

Part of the healing process involves remembering that God is present in all that happens in our lives, including the hardest parts.

Even if we are not aware, he was carrying us through our trials and surrounding us with his love when we were hurt. And most of all, in his Providence, he can bring good from whatever suffering we have endured.

The Bible most eloquently makes this important point in the story of Joseph, who was sold by his brothers into slavery. At that moment, Joseph lost everything. He was separated from his beloved father, thinking he would never see him again. He was taken far away to Egypt and forced to work as a slave for a man named Potiphar. But even through these trials, when all hope seemed to be lost, the Bible two times underscores an important reality: *"The* Lord *was with Joseph. ... The* Lord *was with him"* (Genesis 39:2–3, emphasis added). God blessed the work of Joseph and gave him favor in the eyes of his master who put Joseph in charge of all his affairs. Though painfully separated from home, he was beginning to find a new life and a new purpose as God was blessing him in Egypt. Joseph was not abandoned. The Lord was with him.

But Joseph faced tragic hardship a second time. When he was falsely accused of trying to seduce Potiphar's wife, Joseph was thrown into an Egyptian prison. He had lost everything all over again. But once more, even in the midst of this dark moment, the Bible tells us twice again, *"The* Lord *was with Joseph. ... The* Lord *was with him"* (Genesis 39:21–23, emphasis added). God blessed him and gave him favor in the eyes of the jailkeeper, who recognized Joseph to be a trustworthy man and put Joseph in charge of all the prisoners.

Eventually, Joseph was released from prison and rose to become Pharaoh's right-hand man, managing the day-to-day affairs of the kingdom. His greatest achievement was stockpiling grain in Egypt to prepare for seven years of famine that he foresaw would come. When the terrible food shortage hit the land, Egypt was not only prepared to feed its own people but also helped many from the surrounding areas find food in this time of starvation.

Some of those people traveling to Egypt to benefit from Joseph's stockpiles were his own brothers who had sold him into slavery many years ago. In a dramatic reunion with his brothers, Joseph explained to them how God was always present, and how God took their evil deed and used it for good—to bring Joseph to Egypt, so he could work with Pharaoh to store up the grain to save many people's lives during the famine. Rejoicing in the magnificence of God's providence that can bring good out of evil, Joseph said to his brothers, "God sent me before you to preserve for you a remnant on earth, and to keep alive for you many survivors. So it was not you who sent me here, but God" (Genesis 45:7–8). And "You meant evil against me; but God meant it for good, to bring it about that many people should be kept alive, as they are today" (Genesis 50:20).

From this story, we see two important points. First, God never abandons his children. Joseph was never abandoned. At every step of the way, "The LORD was with Joseph. ... The LORD was with him." Second, if God allows a certain hardship to unfold in our lives, we should trust that he can bring good out of it. We saw earlier that none of us can escape suffering. All disease, disaster, conflict, violence, neglect, and harm entered this world because of human sin. But as the *Catechism* explains, "God in his almighty providence can bring a good from the consequences of an evil, even moral evil, cause by his creatures" (CCC 312). Indeed, God used the greatest evil of all time—the murder of his innocent beloved Son—to bring about the greatest good, our salvation.

Entrusting the Past to God

Notice what St. Paul says: "In everything God works for good with those who love him" (Romans 8:28). The key word is *everything*. Paul doesn't say "in some cases" or "in the good parts of our lives" but in absolutely everything—the good, the bad, the ugly, the messy, the challenging, and the painful—"God works for good with those who love him." So no matter what we have endured in life, we should trust that God can and is always working good from it for us.

After all, we can't change the past. So there's no use in resisting it, complaining about it, or making ourselves bitter about it. It's also not healthy to pretend it never happened, deny it doesn't affect us, or suppress it deep into our subconsciousness. The past is an event that occurred in our lives. And the one thing we can do with the past is use our freedom to name it, surrender to it, embrace it, and entrust it to God, trusting that he can use it for some good for us or for others.

This is the beauty of human freedom. We cannot change the fact that we have been hurt or have lost something. But we can turn our hurt or our loss into an opportunity to love. Whatever has been taken away from us by other people or through the events in our lives can be freely offered as a gift to the Lord. All that we have lost through suffering—our plans, our possessions, our time, our health, our physical and emotional well-being, our reputation, our being treated with dignity—all we have lost can be turned into a freely offered sacrifice to the Lord, a gift of love and trust, a sacrifice we can offer as Jesus offered himself on the Cross. And when we do that, we become more like Christ himself. Over time, those wounded parts of our lives become resurrected, they don't weigh us down like they used to, and we become free to be more of our true selves, fully alive in Christ. The wounds are still there, but they are like the glorified wounds in Jesus' hands and side on Easter—they no longer cause the pain they did on Good Friday and can even become something beautiful—a beautiful source of grace for our own lives and healing for others.

We cannot change what has already happened, but we can transform how that past event affects us interiorly. We can transform it into trust and love. This does not change what occurred or fix all the problems in the world outside of us. But it does profoundly change the attitude in our soul. It transforms our hearts from within.

As Father Jacques Philippe explains, "We are not always masters of the unfolding of our lives, but we can always be masters of the meaning we give them. Our freedom can transform any event in our lives into an expression of love, abandonment, trust, hope, and offering. The most important and most fruitful acts of our freedom are not those by which we transform the outside world as those by which we change our inner attitude in light of the faith that God can bring good out of everything without exception."[90]

* * * * * *

Why do you think Jesus wants to heal not just our sins but also the wounds we have suffered in life? Ask Jesus for his healing power to touch our entire lives, healing even whatever wounds we have suffered, healing them in according to his timetable and in whatever way he deems best.

24

Nothing But My Beloved

Bride to the Beloved:
You looked with love upon me
And deep within your eyes imprinted grace
this mercy set me free,
held in your love's embrace,
to lift my eyes adoring to your face.
– St. John of the Cross[91]

The writings of the sixteenth-century Spanish mystic St. John of the Cross can appear intimidating to many modern readers: thick, impersonal, difficult to understand, and even more difficult to live. But when seen in the context of his life and his overall spiritual theology, we can appreciate why his works are considered some of the most important spiritual texts in the Catholic tradition. They flow from the heart of man who was passionately in love with God and urgently wanted to do all he could to remove all obstacles in his spiritual life and arrive at a deeper union with the Lord, like a bride ardently longing to be united with her Beloved.

In the next three reflections, we will touch on only a few of his many profound insights.[92] But even a brief introduction to these themes is important. These themes can make all the difference between souls who allow themselves to be led by God to the next level in the spiritual life and those souls who plateau—who keep doing good Christian things on the outside but are too attached interiorly to their own will and never take that next serious step of union with God.

Infinite Caverns

The first key point we will consider is the theme of *infinite caverns of longing*. St. John of the Cross wants us to be aware of the deepest desires on the human soul. He says the soul has great caverns that are infinitely deep because they are made for God. Specifically, he says the human memory, intellect, and will are like infinite caverns—infinite holes in our souls—that only God can fill. "They are as deep as the boundless goods of which they are capable, since anything less than the infinite fails to fill them."[93]

Our problem is that we try to fill these caverns with the things of this world: success, wealth, the pleasures of food, drink, and sex, a certain plan, a certain dream, a certain status, more possessions, more approval, more applause. These things are not bad in themselves, but they cannot satisfy. They become a problem when we put them at the center of our lives—when we seek them to fulfill us or strive to find our identity and security in them. As St. Augustine famously wrote, "Our hearts are restless until they rest in you, O Lord."[94]

Though most of us might nod and acknowledge this truth in our minds—that only God can satisfy the deepest longings on our hearts—why do we still run after praise, wealth, pleasure, the need to control? And why do we do it over and over again? John of the Cross would answer that it's because many of us (even devout, committed Christians) tend to live on the surface of our spiritual lives. We are not in tune enough with those innermost desires in the caverns of our soul. We tend to seek immediate comforts and satisfactions and are too afraid or too distracted to go deeper with God in prayer. So we settle for many things that are less than God.

Nada

This leads to a second key theme for John of the Cross: *nada*. John uses the word *nada* (which in Spanish means "nothing") several times to describe the importance of asceticism, the traditional spiritual practice of making sacrifices and voluntarily denying oneself of comforts, pleasures, and all tendencies to selfishness. Consider the following few excerpts from a famous passage in his book *The Ascent of Mount Carmel*. But get ready. These lines, taken on their own, might seem a bit overwhelming:

> Strive always to prefer, not that which is easiest, but that which is most difficult;
>
> Not that which gives most pleasure, but rather that which gives least;
>
> Not that which is restful, but that which is wearisome;
>
> Not that which is a desire for anything, but that which is a desire for nothing;
>
> Strive thus to desire to enter into complete detachment and emptiness and poverty with respect to everything that is in the world, for Christ's sake.[95]

Wow, that sounds intense! To prefer always what is most difficult and least pleasurable, to desire nothing and to become completely detached from this world—that might seem, at first glance, quite inhuman. Is it possible, or even desirable, for a Christian to live that way? But there's more. Consider a few other thought-provoking lines from this work:

> In order to arrive at having pleasure in everything, desire to have pleasure in nothing.
>
> In order to arrive at the possessing of everything, desire to possess nothing.

In order to arrive at being all,
desire to be nothing.

To come to the knowledge of all,
desire to know nothing.[96]

Admittedly, these lines can be intimidating. But we should not view his spirituality as some harsh, cold path of rigid self-denial or some arduous climb up a mountain of perfection achieved only by renouncing all human desire. When viewed within in the larger framework of John of the Cross' life and writings, will see that his no—his *nada*—is far from a rejection of human desire. It's more about a *yes* to the soul's desires: to its truest, deepest desires. It's about saying no to lesser things in order to create more space for greater things. Indeed, his emphasis on *nada* is about making more space in our lives in order to be more in tune with those infinite longings in the caverns of our soul—and with the only One who can fill them.

Take, for example, a young person falling in love. He might spend less time with his friends, family, work, and hobbies in order to have more time to spend with his beloved. It is love that is impelling him to say no to these other things so that he can say yes to spending more time with her. Similarly, St. John of the Cross is inviting us to give less time, energy, and attention to money, status, screens, frivolous entertainments, and the honors, comforts, and delights of this world so that we can have more space in our hearts to seek our heart's deepest desire, our Beloved, Jesus.

Hands Already Full

St. John of the Cross uses the analogy of someone's hands being full. Such a person is not able to receive what God wants to give them. I think of my wife holding a child in one arm and some groceries in the other and then another one of our children coming to her, saying, "Here, Mommy, hold my soccer ball for me!" There's not enough room to hold the ball at that moment; her hands are already full.

This is what happens when we cling to the things we think we need to be happy: our preferences, comfort, career, human praise, health, a certain position, a certain plan, a certain relationship, a certain vision we have for our children, the pleasures of food, drink, or sex. We cling to our own will. But when we grip tightly to what we want all the time, our hands aren't fully open to receive what God wants to give, which, ultimately, is himself. John of the Cross explains that there are some Christians who "do not stay empty so that God might fill them with his delight. ... Their hands are already full and they could not take what God was giving."

How about you? What are you attached to? What are you clinging to right now that might be keeping you from having open hands to receive what God wants to give you? Consider these words from John of the Cross: "Remain empty ... out of love for Christ."[97] Notice how his *nada*—his call to remain empty and to say no to lesser things—is all about love. It's not about self-renunciation for its own sake. He says, "Remain empty ... *out of love for Christ*." It's *love* that impels us to want to say no to other things in order to make more room for Jesus.

In another passage, he explains it this way: "Say no to your desires and you'll discover what your heart really desires."[98] This is what the *nada* is all about. It's not about cold-hearted detachment, rigid self-control, or the suppression of all desire. It's more about the passionate desire of a lover who runs after his Beloved and urgently does all he can to make more and more room in his soul for the One he loves. Indeed, the *nada*, the nothing of John of the Cross is about making sure that there is no-thing—no relationship, no plan, no possession, no worldly praise, honor, comfort, or pleasure—that takes the place of "the one thing" that our soul infinitely desires.

Loving Detachment

It is crucial we work on rooting out our attachments. The things to which we're attached weigh us down in the spiritual life. Whatever we cling to prevents us from growing in deeper union with the Lord. Many good, believing Christians start growing in the spiritual life but plateau and become mediocre because they do not seriously strive to deny themselves regularly and break from their attachments. They might do many good Catholic things: they pray, they are involved at their parish, they participate in a small group, they follow the teachings of the Catholic Church. But they remain attached to various comforts, pleasures, and plans for their own lives. St. John of the Cross points out that, in the long term, these attachments are more damaging to our spiritual lives than certain weaknesses or even occasional venial sins—for our attachments habitually hinder our will and our desires, directing them away from the One thing that will satisfy and toward something less than God.

Consider the following passage from John of the Cross that demonstrates why we must urgently strive to conquer our attachments, even if they are not sinful attachments, lest they keep us from our desire for God. In his analogy, our sins are likened to a cord that holds a bird down, preventing it from flying to the heights, while our attachments are only a thin thread. But both the small thread and the strong cord keep the bird from soaring.

> It makes little difference whether a bird is tied by a thin thread or by a cord. Even if it is tied by thread, the bird will be held bound just as surely as if it were tied by a cord; that is, it will be impeded from flying as long as it does not break the thread. Admittedly the thread is easier to break, but no matter how easily this may be done, the bird will not fly away without first doing so. This is the lot of those who are attached to something. No matter how much virtue they have they will not reach the freedom of the divine union.[99]

This is the challenge: even if we have overcome various sins from our past and have cultivated many virtues and pious practices over the years, we still will be held back significantly in our spiritual life if we don't strive to conquer our many attachments, *even to things that are not sinful*. Remember, anything less than God will not satisfy. So if we cling to some pleasure, comfort, dream, or status—if we don't aggressively root out our habit of impure thoughts and glances, our attachment to having food or drink whenever we want, or our attachment to screens and social media—our hands will not be open to receive God himself. We will habitually seek to fill the caverns of our soul with lesser things that distract us from our deepest, truest desires.

This is why we must seriously strive to break from our various attachments, denying ourselves and picking up our cross each day, so that no-thing takes the place of the *one* thing necessary: Jesus (see Luke 10:42). As John of the Cross explains, without the regular practice of self-denial, all other virtues and spiritual practices "would amount to no more than going around in circles without getting anywhere. ... I would not consider any spirituality worthwhile that wants to walk in sweetness and ease and run from the imitation of Christ."[100]

What does the practice of self-denial look like? It will be different for each person, but here are some examples:

- We can train ourselves not to delight in or even be curious about an impure image that pops up on a screen. We must guard our eyes and not look lustfully at another person. We must also guard our thoughts and imagination and keep our hearts pure.

- It is also good to deny ourselves our favorite food or drink on occasion, cultivating the interior freedom to say no and not consume what we crave. Fasting, not eating between meals, eating simply, eating less, being willing to eat what we don't like, not having to fill our stomachs at every moment of hunger—these are other ways to grow in our detachment from the pleasures of food and drink.

- Other practices include making sacrifices; giving in to others' preferences; letting others have their way; enduring misunderstandings and not defending yourself; holding back when you tend to dominate conversation; being obedient and submitting to a superior or a family member's request even when you don't want to; accepting the discomfort of heat, cold, hunger, and tiredness; and remaining joyful, not complaining even in our own thoughts when we don't get our way.

- In our digital age, we must also cultivate interior freedom in regard to our screens, phones, and devices: not having to look at every message, update, or notification; not having to scroll through social media posts and stories; taking periodic fasts from our screens; being free to live without our device on occasion; and not looking at screens before bed. Do you have this kind of interior freedom from screens and social media?

These are only a few examples of the kinds of self-denial that help break our attachments to the things of this world and create more space in our soul for God.

But there's an even deeper level of detachment and purification of our desires that we need, and ultimately it is not something we can achieve on our own. God needs to intervene in a significant way in order to get to the very roots of our many attachments. How God does this is what we will consider next.

* * * * * *

In prayer, reflect on what attachments you have. Is there a certain comfort, plan, relationship, or dream that you cling to and seek for your identity and happiness? Ask God to show you. And ask him for the grace to help entrust that part of your life to him more fully and to make more space in your heart for him.

25

Darkness

On a cold night in December 1577, armed men raided the room of St. John of the Cross, blindfolded him, handcuffed him, and carried him off as a prisoner to be interrogated and then flogged. He disappeared, and no one knew where he was taken.

His fellow Carmelites who had been part of a reform movement he was leading were worried. John and his counterpart St. Teresa of Avila had been calling the Carmelite friars and nuns in Spain to a deeper commitment to prayer, poverty, and sacrifice. The movement had been gathering momentum and bearing much fruit. But now John was gone, and no one knew where he was.

Though Teresa did not know where John was, she knew who had taken him away. It was the other Carmelites, who opposed the reform and resented Teresa and John for it. Teresa wrote to the King of Spain, pleading with him to find the saint and rescue him. "I would be happier if [he] had fallen into the hands of the Moors—they might show [him] more pity."[101]

The other Carmelites took the idea of reform as a criticism of their way of life. So they kidnapped John and took him to Toledo, Spain, where he was thrown into a prison cell for two months. Then, even worse, they locked him away in a narrow room, only six by ten feet, with just one tiny two-inch-wide window up high. He was given barely anything to eat, just bread and water. There he sat—hungry, in the dark, in solitary confinement—for seven long months.

His cell was frigid in the winter and suffocating in the hot summer. He endured regular floggings that left scars on his body for many years. He later wrote, "I've been flogged more than St. Paul!"[102] He wore the same unwashed clothing for the entire period and suffered with lice. The worst part, however, was the psychological torture. Guards would stage conversations outside his cell about his death, saying that the only way he was getting out was in a casket. He lived in constant fear that his food might be poisoned. He had to deal with the never-ending accusation that he was a rebel and that his reform was not from God. His greatest fear was that Teresa and the others might think he had given up on the reform and abandoned them.

Close to death, John attempted a dangerous escape. He loosened the screws of his lock when the guards were away. Then at night, when the friars were all asleep, he pushed the door hard, and the lock came loose. He made a kind of rope out of torn strips of his bed covers, escaped out the window and scaled down the wall. He eventually found refuge in one of the Teresian convents who had supported their reform.

The sisters were shocked by his appearance. He looked like a dead man. They went to the chapel together to pray in thanksgiving for his escape. The sisters sang a hymn about love and suffering that included the following line: "He who knows nothing of pains in this valley of sorrows, knows nothing of good things nor has tasted of love, since pains are the garment of lovers."[103] At this hymn, John motioned for them to stop singing. He grabbed the grail and leaned his head against it, trembling and weeping. He stayed like that, weeping, for one hour.

Light in Darkness

God sometimes uses difficult events in our lives, darkness in prayer, and intense dryness in the spiritual life to heal us at the deepest levels of our soul. That certainly was the case with St. John of the Cross. During his torturous imprisonment, he was pushed to the limits of suffering. But his worst pain was not the physical and psychological torture or the loneliness and fear he felt while sitting in the darkness of his cell for those seven long months. There was a more devastating *inner* darkness he experienced in his soul. During his ordeal the Lord withdrew a sense of his closeness to John, precisely in this period when John seemed to need it most. In this spiritual darkness, he cried out with an ache and longing for God as never before:

> Where have you hidden,
> Beloved, and left me groaning?
> You fled like a stag
> having wounded me;
> I went out in search of you, and you were gone.[104]

This is the first stanza of one of the poems John composed while in prison—writings hailed as some of the best verses in Spanish literature. John himself said some of it was from God. The poem expresses John's passionate, painful longing to find God in the midst of his severe darkness. This cry, awakened from the depths of his soul, serves as a window into his interior life and points to the beautiful wisdom he has to offer us regarding an important work God wants to do in all who love him.

Think about what happened to him. In those seven months, John was stripped of all that was dear to him: of all friends, comforts, freedoms, and pleasures of this world; of whatever sense of achievement he might have had from the reform movement he was helping lead; and of any praise or gratitude for his work. Most of all, he was stripped of any consolation in prayer and a sense of God's closeness. Over time, however, he came to see God was not far away, but was very close—perhaps uncomfortably close, even painfully close—but doing the deepest work in his soul.

Before we consider the next theme in John's spiritual theology, let's briefly recall what we've seen so far:

- *Deep caverns:* Our souls have infinite caverns only God can fill.

- *But our hands are full:* God can't fill us if our hands are full, if we are too attached to the pleasures and comforts of this world or clinging to certain things, people, or dreams to be our security and make us happy.

- *Detachment and making space:* Our attachments prevent us from deeper union with God. That's why so much of the spiritual life is about making space in our souls for God—to be more in tune with the deepest desires on our heart, which are for him. We say no to lesser things—even various attachments that are not sinful—in order to say yes to God.

Now, we're ready to see how John of the Cross goes one significant step further. He underscores how this process of "saying no" to our attachments and "making space" for God is not something we can do by ourselves. No matter what we do with our own effort, we cannot purify ourselves enough on our own. There are some disordered desires and emotions that run so deep in us they require a significant divine intervention. There are some attachments and defects that only God can heal when he gets beyond our deliberate control. As the saint explains, "No matter how much individuals do through their own efforts, they cannot actively purify themselves enough to be disposed in the least degree for the divine union of the perfection of love. God must take over and purge them in that fire that is dark for them."[105] And he will use the circumstances of our lives, the difficult trials we face, the suffering, and even the withdrawal of a sense of his presence to get to the root of our sins and weaknesses.

Weaning

Second, St. John of the Cross uses an analogy from family life to explain this point. He says God cares for a soul like a mother nurtures a small child. At first, God nurses the soul with sweet milk, giving the person intense satisfaction and consolation in all spiritual practices. Going deeper in the Catholic Faith is exciting. The soul finds joy in lengthy prayers, delight in making sacrifices, and excitement about frequenting the sacraments. God infuses spiritual practices with his sweetness to draw the soul closer to him.

But God wants to take us deeper. In these early stages, souls might carry out good spiritual activities, but not for the right reasons. They might pray, go to Adoration, go to Mass, consume a lot of Catholic content, and participate in a small group. It's all new, exciting, and enriching. But their motivation is less about God himself and more about getting some benefit for themselves, some feeling, consolation, or sense of community and purpose. Those are not bad in themselves, but they are not God. The Lord wants to wean us from these natural goods—fellowship, a sense of direction in life, delight in prayer, joy in learning about the Faith, a sense of progressing spiritually—so that we can be disposed to receive the greatest spiritual good of all, which is God himself.

That's why the Lord sometimes uses difficult circumstances in life and a new, prolonged spiritual dryness to wake up the soul and draw it out of this beginner's state. John says it is like a mother weaning her child and putting it down so it can learn to walk on its own two feet:[106] "There, through pure dryness and interior darkness, He weans them from the breasts of these gratifications and delights, takes away all these trivialities and childish ways, and makes them acquire the virtues by very different means. No matter how earnestly beginners in all their actions and passions practice the mortification of self, they will never be able to do so entirely—far from it—until God accomplishes it in him passively by means of the purgation of this night."[107]

When a child first is forced to go without his mother's milk, he is utterly terrified. The same happens when the mother puts the child down to learn how to walk. The child kicks and screams and does not understand why this is happening to him. "Why can't I have my mother's sweet milk?" the child wonders. "Why can't my mother hold me now?" But the mother knows it is good for the child to learn to eat solid food and learn to walk on his own. And God does the same for the beginner. He takes away all spiritual delight and comfort in order to draw the soul to a deeper level of the spiritual life. But this is completely disorienting and painful for the soul. God "weans them from the sweet breast so that they might be strengthened ... and puts them down from His arms that they may grow accustomed to walking by themselves. This change is a surprise to them because everything seems to be functioning in reverse."[108]

People will go through various trials, sorrows, and darkness throughout life, even in the spiritual life. All that is a usual part of living in this fallen world, in this "valley of tears." But how does a soul know if it might be going through this kind of deeper purification and darkness that John of the Cross describes? And what should a soul do if it ever finds itself in this situation? We will turn to these questions in the next reflection.

* * * * * *

Ask God to reveal to you a place in your life where he might be "weaning" you off of a former way of praying and giving you more solid food for maturity. Ask him to help you trust him in the new ways he may be leading you. Ask him to help make this new way of love delightful to you and surrender your growth in maturity to him.

26

Three Signs in the Darkness

It is a bit unsettling to stand in total darkness—in a dark basement when the lights go out or when wandering from your campsite on a pitch-black night and your flashlight gives out. In the darkness of night, we cannot see. We do not know exactly where we are and where we are going. We do not know what might be coming toward us. The thick darkness is all around us—we cannot stop it. We can only accept it. We are not in control.

That is one of the lessons darkness teaches us and why St. John of the Cross turned to this image so often: we are not in control. When God draws very close to us, it can be uncomfortable. For souls not ready to welcome him at this deeper level, for souls who have not made enough space for him, his drawing near is unsettling. God is pressing in to make space for his presence, to make room in the soul for the inflow of his healing love. John describes how, for these souls, the fire of his love is not experienced as something gentle, but afflictive. God is trying to teach the soul to know and love him in a new way. But that can be completely bewildering, for we like to be in control. We like to be the ones charting our course in life, including our spiritual life. But much to our dismay, we are left in the dark.

Darkness

When thrown into spiritual darkness, we might fear we are going backward in the spiritual life. Our normal habits of prayer are not working like they used to. It's dry. We're bored. God seems distant. The methods and books we previously enjoyed using don't work for us anymore, no matter how hard we try. Our prayer life is not just more difficult. It's completely turned upside down.

Life situations also take a dramatic turn. A friendship is strained. We are uncertain about the future. We are sick. We are terribly lonely. Our normal patterns of flourishing—how we find our self-worth, our identity, our meaning and purpose in life—are not working like they used to. Life isn't just more difficult. We feel completely unsettled, disoriented, and unsure where our life is going.

Every Christian regularly faces ups and downs, trials and disappointments, and even periods of dryness and frustration in prayer. That's normal. That doesn't mean you are in a dark night of the soul. You could just be having a rough season in life. The dark night is something more.

St. John of the Cross tells us there are three signs a soul may be experiencing a dark night. First, there is no satisfaction in anything—friendships, work, leisure, hopes for the future, prayer, sacraments, spiritual reading, or Christian fellowship. Second, the soul has great concern that it is not serving God well, that it is slipping spiritually. The soul is not lukewarm or careless in its spiritual life. It earnestly seeks to follow God and is very concerned that it has done something wrong and is going backward in its walk with the Lord. Third, the soul is powerless to do meditative prayer. It is persevering in daily prayer and sincerely trying to do some kind of meditation (whether *lectio divina*, Ignatian contemplation, or some other type of meditative prayer). But no matter how hard it tries, there are no consolations. Nothing seems to be working well at all.

What to Do?

What should a soul do if it finds itself in a genuine dark night? First, resist the temptation to run away from the darkness. Fight against the panicked inclination to seek comfort and satisfaction in your former ways of praying. God is inviting you to something new: a more divinely infused contemplation. St. John of the Cross says active meditation is useless now because God is leading the soul along a new path of prayer.[109]

Second, persevere in prayer but in a more receptive way. Continue making time for prayer each day. But be open to your prayer being different. Allow your soul to rest in quiet and solitude with God, even if it seems you're wasting time or not accomplishing much. John says to be content simply with "a loving and peaceful attentiveness to God."[110] You may not be able to *feel* God's presence, but you still can rest in prayer, confident he is there with you in the darkness. You should not try to stir up some feeling, for that will only make your situation more difficult. "Live without the concern, without the effort, and without the desire to taste or feel Him. All these desires disquiet the soul and distract it from the peaceful quiet and sweet idleness of the contemplation that is being communicated to it. ... The more a person seeks some support in knowledge and affection the more the soul will feel the lack of these."[111]

During this period, people shouldn't be worried if they are not using their minds to reflect on the Scriptures or mysteries of the Faith or if their emotions are not stirred or if they do not come away with some profound insight or practical resolution in prayer. God is preparing them for something new. The main concern is to accept sitting in the darkness and receive what God is giving them. They should make sure that "they themselves may be no obstacle to the operations of the infused contemplation that God is bestowing, that they may receive it with more peaceful plentitude and make room in their spirits for the enkindling and burning of the love that this dark and secret contemplation bears and communicates to the soul. For contemplation is nothing else than a secret and peaceful and loving inflow of God, which, if not hampered, fires the soul in the spirit of love."[112]

> One dark night,
> Fired with love's urgent longings
> —ah, the sheer grace!—
> I went out unseen,
> My house being now all stilled.[113]

* * * * * *

Take some time to simply rest in God's presence, trusting that he's there whether you can feel his presence or not. Simply let your "house be stilled."

Part Seven

IN THE WORLD, NOT OF THE WORLD

27

Into the Silence

St. Benedict of Nursia lived in a time of cultural crisis. Straddling the fifth and sixth centuries, he experienced the collapse of the great Roman Empire and the resulting social, political, and moral upheaval as the institutions and values that had held Rome together for centuries crumbled and barbarian peoples invaded the land.

Coming from a wealthy family in Norcia—a town about one hundred miles from Rome—Benedict was sheltered from much of the instability in the city and had a relatively normal childhood. But when his parents sent him to Rome to study, he stepped with one foot into the chaotic culture around him, witnessing the debauchery of Rome and the decadent lifestyles of his fellow students. Benedict did not want to make the same mistakes. He only wanted to please God. So he left his studies, took a step back from the negative influences of the city, and withdrew to the quiet mountains east of Rome, where he lived in solitude in a cave at Subiaco for three years. As his first biographer, St. Gregory the Great, put it, "He drew back his foot, which he had as it were now set forth into the world, lest, entering too far in acquaintance with it, he likewise might have fallen into that dangerous and godless gulf."[114]

Benedict was humble enough to admit that the culture around him in Rome affected him. He didn't say, "I'm okay. It's not a big deal. The culture doesn't influence me." He didn't underestimate how the values and lifestyles of the world often lure even practicing Christians to follow its standards instead of Christ's. So he wisely stepped back and chose to live a very different kind of life.

How about you? Are you aware of the ways the culture of our own day might be impeding your prayer life and your growth as a Christian? Do you ever consider how might God be inviting you to give up something that is common in the mainstream world around us but not healthy for a true Christian disciple? Though most of us are not called to live as hermits like St. Benedict did, we're all called to take seriously what St. Paul said to the Christians living in the pagan world of his day: "Do not be conformed to this world but be transformed by the renewal of your mind" (Romans 12:2).

Stepping Aside

By stepping out of the mainstream culture, Benedict could experience a deeper personal renewal in Christ and become a source of renewal for the world around him. Indeed, St. Benedict is recognized as one of the most influential people the world has ever known, helping shape much of Europe and Christian culture for centuries. His famous *Rule* and the hundreds of Benedictine monasteries founded throughout Europe became a great light in a time of great darkness, offering men and women an alternative way of life—a life in Christ—that was more enduring than anything the chaotic world around them was offering.

We are living in times not unlike those of St. Benedict, as many of the basic Christian values that held Western Civilization together for centuries are often questioned, dismantled, and set aside. St. Benedict has much to offer us today in our own world that is becoming less and less Christian. How should we live as Christians in a secular culture? How much of the world should we take in? How much should we avoid? How do we live *in* the world, but not be of the world? Let's consider just two of the many important themes from the life of St. Benedict that can apply to us Christians today. Let's reflect on the need for more silence and interior stillness in our lives.

Silence

First, if we want to hear God's voice in prayer, we need to build more silence into our daily lives. For modern men and women, however, that sounds very scary. Silence? We fill our days with constant noise and distraction. Music in the car. Music in our earbuds. Music in our kitchens. We fill our heads with videos, podcasts, sports, the news, shows, and movies. We are constantly clicking through endless stories, reels, and posts. Silence is something the modern man wants to avoid! We are uncomfortable with ourselves and dread being left alone with our own thoughts. So we keep the noise, music, and screens on all around us. And if we ever do find ourselves alone for a just moment, with nothing to do—God forbid!—we instinctively pull out our phones to distract ourselves lest we have to think about our life, look at nature, or rest in the presence of the Lord in silence.

Consider what the nineteeth century Danish philosopher Søren Kierkegaard once said: "If I were a doctor and I could prescribe just one remedy for all the ills of the modern world, I would prescribe silence. For even if the Word of God were proclaimed in the modern world, no one would hear it, because of the panoply of noise. Therefore, *create silence.*"[115] What's most noteworthy about this quotation is the fact that it comes from the 1800s—long before radio, TV, computer screens, phones, and the many other devices that hinder us from meeting God in the silence of our hearts. Imagine what Kierkegaard would say today!

If we want to encounter God more profoundly in prayer, we need to unplug from our devices—not just in the chapel, but many times throughout the day. This is a crucial point: *how we live the rest of the day impacts our prayer time.* If we fill the rest of the day with noise and constant activity, we are more likely to be distracted and restless during prayer. We'll find ourselves humming a song on our playlist, thinking of a scene from a show, or picturing something from social media. If that's what we fill our minds with throughout the day, that's what we'll bring into our time with God in prayer.

Can we build in some silence at different points throughout the day? When we're waiting in line, waiting to pick up the kids, waiting at a red light—do we always need to pull out our phones in these moments? If we can't sit quietly with our thoughts in those small pauses in our day, how can we be fully present to God in silent prayer? In those little pockets of space in our day, resisting the pull to grab our phones may be one of the most heroic spiritual choices we make we make in our daily lives. Indeed, choosing to remain in silence or choosing to grab our rosary beads rather than our phones can do wonders for preparing ourselves to be present to God in prayer.

We need to have a certain distance, a detachment from it all. We need to cultivate interior space in our hearts to be in possession of our own thoughts, to be more aware of ourselves, of others, of God's presence around us, and most of all, of what God may be doing in our soul moment to moment throughout the day. As Mother Teresa once said, "We need to find God, and he cannot be found in noise and restlessness. God is the friend of silence. See how nature—trees, flowers, grass—grow in silence; see the stars, the moon and the sun, how they move in silence. ... The more we receive in silent prayer, the more we can give in our active life."[116]

Think of all the unnecessary time we spend on our devices throughout the day—every message, interruption, update, story, video, and post. It's not just wasting time. It's much worse than that. It's hurting our souls. It's preventing us from giving our attention to what matters most in life: our children, spouse, friends, and our interior lives with God.

And the constant distraction is also keeping us from being the kind of person who is receptive to the Lord, attentive to the presence of God throughout the day. It inhibits us from noticing the movements of Christ in our heart, responding to the promptings of the Spirit, and hearing the voice of God. How many times a day does Our Lord say, "I stand at the door and knock; if anyone hears my voice and opens the door, I will come in to him" (Revelation 3:20)? How many times do we fail to hear his voice because we never cultivate silence in our soul? God's voice is drowned out by so much unnecessary noise because staying connected on social media is more important to us than staying connected with the Lord throughout the day.

Let's remember the example of St. Benedict"s withdrawal into silence and carve out times in the day, spaces in our soul, to step aside from all the noise and distraction. Let's intentionally pull back from it and cultivate an ongoing quiet place in our souls, an inner cell we keep with us throughout the day where can hear the voice of Jesus, open the door of our hearts, and let him in.

Activity Versus Interior Peace

Second, St. Benedict withdrew from the fury of worldly activity in Rome to focus on "the one thing necessary": Christ. Again, we don't need to become hermits, but we do need to recognize how the pressure and pace of our modern world is often not human and not conducive to an interior life. We are made for more than projects, work, and accomplishments. There is much more to life than going to meetings in the office, responding to messages, shuttling kids to their dozen activities, keeping your inbox empty, and completing to-do lists. The pressures young people in particular feel to perform well in school, tests, athletics, activities, and competitions are intense. Adults also feel the stress to achieve a lot in their careers, succeed in the workplace, provide for their families, and give their kids the best experiences, education, coaches, lessons, everything. Yet amid all these pressures of the modern age, God says to us, "Be still and know that I am God" (Psalm 46:10).

Do you ever feel so busy that you don't have time to think, rest, plan your day, thoughtfully consider your next steps, and leisurely converse with others? That rapid pace in life is not healthy. It's not human. We are not meant to be like machines constantly producing something. We are meant to be human beings, not "human doings." Unfortunately, we might think our busyness is a sign we are an important person, doing a lot for the company or the kingdom and being responsible in taking care of our family. But the saints would tell us otherwise. Being swept away by incessant activity is likely a sign that we struggle with one of the most deadly vices that can ruin one's spiritual life: sloth.

Yes, sloth! Sloth is not about a lack of activity but the lack of the *right kind* of activity. We are made for union with God. We are made to know and love him, to contemplate his beauty, goodness, and love. Our hearts are restless until they rest in God. The vice that blocks this movement toward God is what the ancients called *acedia*, which is *spiritual* laziness.

The busy Christian who pours himself out at work, at home, and even at the parish, volunteering for the food drive, participating in Bible studies, and attending various retreats and conferences may on the outside look like a very committed disciple. But his bustling activity might be covering up a slackness of spirit. Behind all his Catholic activity and his busyness for his family and career may be lurking a lazy soul who does not take time for what matters most: friendship with God. If someone does not take time for daily prayer, leisure, rest, and introspection, he may be struggling with the vice of sloth. He is not in possession of himself. He is a slave to his impulses to keep busy all the time, to run to the next activity, meeting, message, or item on his to-do list.

St. Bernard of Clairvaux warned the pope in his day to avoid this very danger. He challenged the pope not to allow himself to be carried away by his many activities and "accursed tasks" to be accomplished.

> I fear, lest in the midst of our occupations without number, you may lose hope of ever getting through with them, and allow your heart to harden. It would be very prudent of you to *withdraw from such occupations,* even if it be only for a little while, rather than let them get the better of you, and little by little, lead you where you do not want to go. And where, you will ask, is that? To *indifference. ...* Such is the end to which these *accursed tasks* will lead you; that is, if you keep on as you have begun, giving yourself entirely to them, keeping nothing of yourself, for yourself.[117]

Bernard is not advocating that we don't work hard or avoid taking on a lot of responsibility. His main concern is that we take time to "withdraw from such occupations, even if only for a little while." We, of course, need to take time for prayer each day. That is one good way to withdraw from the frenetic pace of the world. But Bernard is calling us to something more: we also need to take time often *right in the midst of our busy days* to pull back from our work, to pause for some brief moments and be recollected—to be aware of the presence of God, talk to him, thank him for the blessings of the day, tell him we love him, and ask for his help with difficulties we are facing.

We can do this right at our desk in the office, at halftime of your kid's soccer match, while driving children home from school or in the bustling kitchen at home. We can pause, just for a few seconds, and in the depths of our hearts think of God. This is what lovers do. Even in the midst of much busyness, they think of each other throughout the day. If they happen to be in the same place, they might glance across the room, make eye contact, smile at each other. They might hold hands or have a quick embrace, even while quickly moving on to the next thing. We can do the same with God. We can take a second to be aware of in his presence, just for a short moment, while getting the dinner ready. We can tell him we love him as we walk down the hallway in between appointments. We can take a moment in the middle of a meeting to say a short prayer in our heart. No one will notice. But God will. And so will you, for you will be living more in communion with God throughout the day, in greater awareness of him throughout your day, instead of living as if you are disconnected from him outside of your designated prayer times.

This is, in part, what Scripture means when it says we are to pray unceasingly. We may not be able to do non-stop Holy Hours throughout the day, but we can cultivate a deeper, ongoing awareness of God's presence with us and our love for him moment by moment throughout the day. We can simply speak to him and speak the name Jesus with love throughout the day. That's what many Christians throughout the centuries have done in the famous Jesus Prayer, repeating the following words either on their lips or in the heart a thousand times a day: "Lord Jesus Christ, Son of God, have mercy on me, a sinner." Rather than letting our hearts be swept away by the fury of activity around us, we can shape our hearts by the rhythm of prayer.

So as we race throughout the day from one important activity and appointment to the next, St. Bernard warns us to be careful not to throw all of ourselves into our tasks. We must keep something of ourselves—our interior lives, our self-possession, our awareness of God's presence—for ourselves in all that we do.

* * * * * *

What is one area in your life where you are "throwing all of yourself" into your tasks or distractions and the "noise" of the world, not leaving enough space in your soul for God? Ask him to show you one simple resolution you can make to help you step more into silence and into being aware his presence with you throughout the day.

28

"Do Not Be Conformed
to This World"

Do you realize that right now there's a battle going on for your mind, for how you look at reality? It's a battle over fundamental questions such as, Who are you? What brings happiness? What is love? What is beauty? What is success? Is there truth? The secular world is trying to get you to look at life one way while Christ offers a very different perspective.

Do not underestimate how much this constant battle impacts your spiritual life. If we wish to encounter God in prayer, we must constantly be on guard to not give the world and its ways too much space in our soul. As we mentioned in the previous reflection, St. Paul urgently instructed the Christians living in first-century pagan Rome, "Do not be conformed to this world but be transformed by the renewal of your minds" (Romans 12:2). His words apply just as much to us today as we strive to live as Christian disciples in our own pagan, secular culture.

But wait a second—does this mean we can't enjoy the good things of this world? And aren't we called to love the world, reach out to the world, and take in all the good the world offers and use it for the sake of the Gospel? Why would St. Paul be so concerned about Christians being conformed to the world?

The World That Is Both Good and Dangerous

St. John Henry Newman explains that in Scripture there are two senses of "the world." On one hand, the Bible speaks of the "world" when simply referring to the human family, the system of human relationships. God made us as relational beings, dependent on each other. We support ourselves and our families, raise children, converse, trade, educate, assist, govern, and entertain. It's in this sense that the world as the human family is good. God created it. At the climax of Creation, God looked at what he had created and saw that "it was very good" (Genesis 1:31). Even though we sinned, God still loved the world and redeemed it through the blood of Christ. "For God so loved the world that he gave his only-begotten Son, that whoever believes in him should not perish but have eternal life" (John 3:16).

Nevertheless, Newman points out that Christians must be careful with this present world. It is good. God made it and died for it. But it is dangerous to us because we are fallen. The world's innocent pursuits and pleasures are good in themselves, but they are not good for us fallen human beings because they are likely to engross us, "to seduce our wayward hearts from our true and eternal good,"[118] Newman says.

So we need to be very careful about how much time and energy we spend on thinking about our comfort, pleasure, financial security, health, problems at work, honor, recognition, status, influence, ambition, and success. None of these may bad in themselves, but they are likely to distract us from what matters most in life. We can't see the spiritual realm—our immortal souls, our growth in virtue, the presence of the Holy Spirit in us, our growth in holiness. But we can see, hear, and feel the world's praises, honors, pleasures, and treasures. Let us not be overconfident in our ability not to be seduced by worldly pleasure, gain, and glory. Instead, let us humbly recognize how susceptible we are to giving more value to the innocent enjoyments and honors of the world than we should.

The World That Hates Christ

Next, Newman explains there is a second sense of the "the world" in Scripture: the world that hates Christ and his followers. Jesus said, "If the world hates you, know that it has hated me before it hated you ... because you are not of the world, but I chose you out of the world, therefore the world hates you" (John 15:18–19). Jesus is referring here to the fallen world governed by the enemy, the devil: "Now is the judgment of this world, now shall the ruler of this world be cast out" (John 12:31).

Newman explains that in Scripture there is this second sense of the world that is not innocent but "positively sinful." The infection of Adam's sin has spread through the whole of the human family which is influenced by the enemy. This is the part of the world that hates what the Church teaches about caring for the poor, the immigrant, the unborn, and the dying; about marriage, sexuality, divorce, and the definition of marriage; about suffering, sacrifice, moral truth, and our responsibility toward others. In sum, this is the world that puts self-rule, autonomy—the "I'm free to do whatever I want" mentality—as the highest good and hates that there is a God who has a plan for our lives that he calls us to follow. This is the world that walks in the footsteps its master, Lucifer, who rebelled against his Creator and said *Non servium!*—I will not serve.

But some might wonder, "If we believe in God and the Church, what do we faithful Christians have to worry about? How might this second sense of 'the world' enter the hearts of ordinary, good followers of Christ who reject Satan and his evil ways?" In response, Newman gives particular attention to what we allow into our souls through what we read, watch, listen to, and participate in through arts and entertainment. And today, this can be applied to all forms of media: what do we take into our minds and hearts from the shows we watch, the music we listen to, the images we look at, and the influencers we follow.

We must be especially careful today because modern media is not designed to appeal primarily to our minds, which makes it harder for us to discern what to take in and what to keep out. Most forms of media largely aim to bypass our minds and appeal to our passions and emotions. So when we watch a show or a video, we don't have our guard up, filtering what we take in, because our minds are not actively engaged. We are more likely to passively allow something into our soul because it is dressed up in a fun show, a funny movie, an attractive image, or a catchy tune.

But let us bring our minds to all we take in through the media: What is the vision for life, success, and happiness being presented? How does the media I consume portray beauty, truth, and goodness? Do I really want to let this vision into my soul? What is the vision of love, sex, marriage, and romantic relationships in our favorite movies and shows? Does it portray what Jesus teaches about these fundamental matters? Is it going to help me or make it harder for me to follow God's plan for virtue, friendship, love, and sexuality?

If a stranger showed up at our door and tried to give a rational argument for why adultery and pre-marital sex are okay, why abortion is okay, why immodesty is not a big deal, and why we should all live for ourselves and have no responsibility to care for those in need, we'd probably reject those ideas very quickly. But when those same ideas are presented in an attractive image, story, show, or song, we let down our guard and passively allow them to enter our hearts. We would reject those ideas outright if we were at church or with our Christian friends, but we passively accept them in shows, songs, and stories and so end up welcoming evil into our homes and into our hearts. And we would be quite naive to think that it doesn't affect our souls.

The Battle

This is where the battle with the world takes place the most—in what we allow into our souls. Some people say the problem of evil is "out there" in the culture—in the media, in Hollywood, in the government, in large corporations, in the school systems. Newman, however, underscores how evil grows and spreads in the world because of people, even Christians, who do not shun it in their hearts. "Evil ... has its strength in the human heart; for though we cannot keep from approving what is right in our conscience, yet we love and encourage what is wrong; so that when evil was once set up in the world, it was secured in its seat by the unwillingness with which our hearts relinquish it."[119]

Have you ever had the experience of watching a show and you find yourself, surprisingly, rooting for sin? The main characters, for example, start to fall in love, and you hope they get together even though she's married to someone else? *Woah, wait. That's adultery! Why am I rooting for an adulterous relationship?* We know something is wrong, but we don't outright reject it in our hearts. We know adultery is immoral, but a part of us might root for it in a show. Similarly, we know this song has bad lyrics, but we tell ourselves we don't listen to the words, we just like the music. We know true beauty is not immodest, but we might enjoy staring at that image that pops up on our screen. A Christian living in today's aggressively secular environment must be constantly on guard against the ways the culture is constantly selling us on a certain vision of life, goodness, love, and beauty that undermines our ability to live according to what Jesus teaches about these matters.

This is where the battle with the world takes place the most— not in Congress or at public demonstrations or on social media, but in the human heart. That's where evil takes root. Remember Newman's observation: "Though we cannot keep from approving what is right in our conscience, yet we love and encourage what is wrong."[120] That's how evil finds its presence in this world. It secures its seat "by the unwillingness with which our hearts relinquish it." If we want to be true disciples who grow in prayer and the spiritual life, we must be more careful and discerning about what we take in. And here's why: Whatever we place before our minds becomes a part of us. The images and ideas shape our desires and influence what we seek in life. It is said that we often become like our friends, the people we associate with most. In today's world, we spend a lot of time with "friends" online, on social media, in shows, and from Hollywood. What vision of life are those friends promoting? What kind of person do you want to become? Let us heed St. Paul's important advice: "Whatever is true, whatever is honorable, whatever is just, whatever is pure, whatever is lovely, whatever is gracious, if there is any excellence, if there is anything worthy of praise, think about these things" (Philippians 4:8).

* * * * * *

Ask God to show you an area in your life where you've let your guard down and let the values of the secular world impact your soul—what you desire, what you pursue in life, what you think will make you happy, how you view others, how you view God. Ask him how this might affect your soul. And ask him for the grace to have a "willingness to relinquish it" so that something more true, honorable, just, and pure may take its place on the throne of your heart.

Part Eight

"... AS I HAVE LOVED YOU"

29

Love of Neighbor

St. Catherine of Siena spent three years in almost perpetual solitude at home, living in prayer and intimate conversation with Jesus, talking with him "as one friend to another." But one day, God challenged her to go back out into the world with people, and this was scary for her. She told the Lord she was afraid that if she mingled in society again, she would lose her contemplative spirit. God reassured her that this was not the case. He was actually inviting her to a deeper love:

> I have no intention whatever of parting you from myself, but rather of making sure to bind you to me all the closer by the bond of your love for your neighbor. Remember that I have laid down two commandments of love: love of me and love of your neighbor. ... It is the justice of these two commandments that I want you now to fulfill. On two feet you must walk my way.[121]

The true mark of holiness is a soul that walks on two feet, not one: both love of God *and* love of neighbor. Holiness, according to the saints, is not measured on one foot—by the number of Holy Hours you pray or Rosaries you recite each week. It's not found in the feelings, delights, and insights you receive in prayer. ("I felt so close to God in prayer today. That must mean I'm really growing in holiness now!") And it's not about how much theology you know, how many Catholic activities you participate in, how orthodox or how faithful to the teachings of the Church you are.

Faithfulness to prayer and the Church, of course, are essential. But those are just the basic starting points. The second foot, love of neighbor, is a chief sign of holiness. Are we cooperating with the graces God gives us in Eucharistic Adoration, devotions, and Bible study in such a way that we are becoming more generous, patient, humble, forgiving, and sacrificial with the people around us? Are we loving our spouses, children, colleagues, and friends as Christ has loved us? Are we loving the poor, the sick, the lonely, the suffering? Being changed into Christ's likeness, especially in our love of neighbor, is the true mark of holiness, not the number of good-Catholic boxes we can check off.

Many of us, however, can tend to be spiritual monopods—we are primarily one-footed Christians. We might be very intentional about encountering God in Mass, Confession, prayer time, and various parish and small group activities. We see the importance of these practices and make time for them. But we are not as intentional with the other foot: pursuing God in our love of neighbor. Loving the people around us seems secondary. We know, of course, we should serve others and be kind to them. But we live as if the only place to grow in holiness is in the sacraments and in prayer time. God wants us to meet him, however, not just in the chapel but also in the ordinary circumstances that come up each day with our spouses, our children, our roommates, and our coworkers. It's easy to love God in the quiet, peaceful solitude of the chapel. It's a lot harder to love Jesus in your spouse who is in a bad mood, in your child who is having a meltdown, in your roommate who doesn't keep things clean, in your coworker who completely dropped the ball, in your boss who doesn't understand, or in your colleague who is selfish and hurtful. When we encounter our neighbor's faults and sins, our love of God is put to the test. In those moments, will we still love our neighbor as God loves us?

Virtue Born in Our Neighbor

Life in community is a school of love. It's where we learn to love like God loves. God loves freely and unconditionally, expecting nothing back. When we sin against him, he does not withdraw his love. He continues to love us no matter how unfaithful, ungrateful, unkind, or unthoughtful we may be. Good Friday makes that clear. But do we love the people in our life this way? In our neighbor, we have the unique opportunity to love like God loves us, loving our neighbor freely, expecting nothing back. As God explained to St. Catherine, "This is why I have put you among your neighbors: so that you can do for them what you cannot do for me—that is, love them without any concern for thanks and without looking for any profit for yourself. And whatever you do for them I will consider done for me."[122]

Indeed, though virtue is conceived in God with prayer, it comes to birth in our neighbor.[123] It is in the daily circumstances of life in community that virtue and holiness are tested and forged: will we love our neighbor like God loves us? Do our interactions with others look like Christ's? Do we, for example, love the people in our lives generously, putting their needs before our own interests and comforts? Do we quickly die to our preferences, giving in to what others want? Do we love the people in our lives patiently, even with all their faults and shortcomings, even when they frustrate us, even when they hurt us? Do we avoid complaining about them or looking down on them, judging them in our hearts? Every time we encounter our neighbor's defects, we have the opportunity either to be irritated and withdraw our love for them or to love Jesus in them all the more. Catherine makes clear what we should do: "You should neither diminish nor grudge your love toward others whether they offend you, or whether their love for you, or the joy or profit you gain from it, weakens. Rather, you should love them tenderly, accepting and putting up with their faults."[124]

Love in Action

St. Thérèse of Lisieux made a similar point. She was at first, however, completely overwhelmed by the New Commandment Jesus gave the Apostles at the Last Supper: "Love one another as I have loved you" (John 15:12).

Think about it: It's one thing to follow the Old Testament ideal, "Love your neighbor as yourself" (Leviticus 19:18). But here, Jesus is asking for so much more. He commands us to love like *he* does! God's love is perfect, complete, infinite. So Thérèse wondered, how could a little human soul like hers, weak, finite, and wounded by Original Sin, possibly love as God so perfectly loves? Jesus' New Commandment doesn't seem fair—God seems to be asking for something that is humanly impossible!

And on this point, she was correct: there is no natural way, no human way, to love like God loves. No human person on his own could do this. Still, Thérèse knew that Jesus would never demand the impossible. So while there is no natural way to love like God loves, she realized there must be a supernatural way, a divine way. She came to the conclusion that the only way she could live the New Commandment would be if Jesus himself lived it out through her. She said to the Lord, "Never would I be able to love my sisters as You love them, unless *You*, O my Jesus, *loved them in me*."[125]

This, in fact, was her own experience. When she found herself, much to her surprise, loving her sisters patiently and generously in challenging circumstances when she might have expected herself to respond with frustration or selfishness, she knew her love for them was not all her own. It was Jesus loving them through her. "I feel it," she wrote, "when I am charitable, it is Jesus alone who is acting in me."[126] Growing in holiness consists in cooperating with

Jesus to change our hearts, allowing him to love others through us in a similar way.

Rising Above Our Feelings

One way that St. Thérèse did this was to seek out the most unpleasant souls in her community. Though our tendency might be to avoid such people, Thérèse had a special preference for those who were most difficult to get along with and who thus were neglected the most. Those who are impolite, who are very sensitive, who lack judgment and good manners. She would become kinder and gentler towards those souls in order "to heal the embittered heart which she felt was suffering."[127] She wrote, "I know very well that these moral infirmities are chronic, that there is no hope of a cure, but I also know that my Mother would not cease to take care of me, to try to console me, if I remained sick all my life. ... I must seek out in recreation, on free days, the company of the Sisters who are least agreeable to me in order to carry out with regard to these wounded souls the office of the Good Samaritan."[128]

There was one sister in the convent who particularly bothered Thérèse. Thérèse wrote how this sister was displeasing to her in everything: "In her ways, her words, her character, everything seems *very disagreeable* to me."[129] Have you ever had people like that in your life? Consider how Thérèse responded. She saw more than the difficult personality of this sister. She also saw her as a daughter of God, a holy religious sister, and someone who must be pleasing to the Lord. She realized that God was inviting her to rise above her natural feelings and love this sister as Christ would. So instead of allowing herself to be repelled by this sister, she chose to do for her what she would do for the person she loved most. Thérèse wanted to love this sister and knew that love is not about feelings but willing the good of the other person, choosing to seek what is best for them, no matter what feelings one may have. "Charity must not consist in feelings but in works," she wrote.[130]

So she started praying for this sister every time she encountered her. She would pray and offer to God all of this sister's good qualities. She also went out of her way to spend time with this sister and perform many kind deeds for her. When the sister said something that was hurtful or wrong, Thérèse resisted the temptation to answer back. She chose instead to offer a most friendly smile and change the topic. So lavish was Thérèse's kindness toward this woman that Thérèse's own sibling Marie (who was with her in the convent) said, "I imagine that you love Sister X more than me!"[131] Thérèse simply laughed and shrugged Marie's comment off, giving no impression of the natural aversion she felt toward the sister. In fact, this sister who received Thérèse's many kind attentions once asked her, "What attracts you so much towards me; every time you look at me, I see you smile?"[132] Thérèse replied that she smiled because she was happy to see her—even though, as she explains in her autobiography, she meant this only from a spiritual standpoint!

Notice how Thérèse rose above her natural feelings. She *chose* to love this sister. Love involves the act of the will, choosing to seek what is best for someone else, no matter what feelings we have for them and even if they bother us, disappoint us, hurt us, and do not love us in return. As Thérèse explained, "Charity consists in bearing with the faults of others, in not being surprised at their weakness."[133]

Encountering Christ in the Lepers

Before his conversion, St. Francis of Assisi was repulsed by the sight of lepers. Yet he recounts how "the Lord led me among them."[134] In the early period of his conversion, Francis lived at a lepers' hostel for a while and earned his keep by caring for the lepers there, cleaning their bodies, dressing their wounds, and treating them with dignity as children of God. His experience with the lepers completely transformed him and was a cornerstone in his conversion. He was a changed man. Through his encounter with the lepers, he came to experience and understand the unsightliness of his own sins and God's incredible mercy toward him. "As I went away from them, that which seemed bitter to me was turned into sweetness of soul and body."[135] From then on, he left the ways of the world and began his new way of life, being completely conformed to the Gospel.

One early tradition tells of Francis riding his horse near Assisi and meeting a leper on the road. Inside, he felt repulsed, but he chose to rise above those feelings. He dismounted from his horse and ran to kiss the leper and give him some money. When he got back on his horse, suddenly the leper was nowhere to be seen. It was then that Francis realized it was Jesus. Francis encountered Christ in this leper.

Francis and all the saints remind us how we encounter Christ not just in prayer and in the sacraments but also in our neighbor. How do you respond when you see your neighbor's faults and annoying qualities? People who are difficult to get along with— people who are proud, selfish, overly sensitive, needy, socially awkward, not pleasant to be with—these are the people saints like Francis and Thérèse didn't avoid. They actually sought them out. They chose to rise above their initial feelings and love Jesus in them.

* * * * * *

Ask Jesus to reveal to you one person in your life who he's inviting you to love as he loves—to bear with the faults of others and love them freely without expecting anything back. Ask Jesus how he's calling you to love that particular person and make a resolution with him to be faithful to being an agent of his love for that person, especially in moments when it may be very difficult to do so.

30

Compassion, Not Judgment

St. Catherine of Siena suffered from what she called "a hidden sickness"—a deep seated sin she didn't even realize was a sin. In fact, she thought she was doing something good for the sake of the kingdom.

She had a keen sense of human nature and an ability to notice other people's faults. She might have thought this was a gift given to her by God. But the Lord confronted her, telling her that those insights she received into other people's weaknesses were not coming from him. They were coming from the devil! The devil wanted her to notice people's faults so that, instead of cultivating a Christ-like heart of patience and compassion for them, she would set herself as judge over them.

God told her she was falling into the devil's trap: "You would think you were judging rightly when in fact you were judging wrongly by following what you saw, for often the devil would make you see too much of the truth in order to lead you into falsehood. He would do this to make you set yourself up as judge of other people's spirits and intentions, something of which, as I told you, I alone am judge."[136]

This reproach from God struck Catherine to the core. Repenting of her sin, she admitted to the Lord, "You gave me ... as medicine against a hidden sickness I had not recognized, by teaching me that I can never sit in judgment on any person. ... For I, blind and weak as I was from this sickness, have often judged others under the pretext of working for your honor and their salvation."[137]

More to the Story

What do you do when you notice other people's faults? Is your heart full of gentleness, compassion, mercy, and understanding? Or is your heart quick to critique, judge, and categorize them? "I can't believe my spouse is treating me like this!" "There he goes again, always trying to take the credit." "Wow, *she's* in a mood today." "Do you know what *he* did on the weekend?" "That family's children are never well behaved." "Hmm. She voted for *that* political candidate?"

When we judge others, it's usually because we are only considering isolated facts. We usually don't see the whole story of what's going on in that person's life. And we certainly cannot see the person's intentions. We don't know their background, their situation, how hard they are trying, what they're going through. We don't know their heart.

We've seen how St. Thérèse of Lisieux had great compassion for the most difficult souls in her community. She realized that when we notice someone having a rough moment, there is usually more to the story. God sees the whole story; we don't. God sees the hurts they have experienced and the difficulties they're facing, and he takes all that into consideration. He also sees their sincere desire to be good, their efforts to change, and their sorrow when they fall. We usually don't see all that. Indeed, the devil doesn't want us to see that—for it would inspire us to be more compassionate, like Christ! We are given only a glimpse of the quick temper, the unkind word, the selfish act, or the moment of weakness, and we immediately get frustrated and judge their heart. Thérèse, however, says, "One should always treat others charitably, for very often what we think is negligence is heroic in God's eyes. A sister who is suffering from migrane, or is troubled internally, does more when she does half of what is required of her than another who does it all, but is sound in mind and body."[138]

Oftentimes, it's because of people's upbringing, temperament, lack of formation, or wounds from their past that make it so hard for them to live virtuously in community with others. If we fully understood the heavy burdens many people carry in life, we would respond to their faults with more gentleness and patience. That's what Thérèse did with a particular sister who often hurt and frustrated her. "I assure you that I have the greatest compassion for Sister X. If you knew her as well as I do, you would see that she is not responsible for all of the things that seem so awful to us. I remind myself that if I had an infirmity such as hers, and so defective a spirit, I would not do any better than she does."[139] She also said, "Ah! If you only knew how necessary it is to forgive her, how much she is to be pitied! It is not her fault if she is so poorly gifted."[140]

Feeling the Sick Person's Pain

If we have truly come to terms with our own weakness and sin, we will be less likely to look down on others and judge them. If we have truly experienced God's patience and mercy with us, we naturally will have more compassion when we notice others' faults. As Pope Francis explains, "The more conscious we are of our wretchedness and our sins, the more we experience the love and infinite mercy of God among us, and the more capable we are of looking upon the many 'wounded' we meet along the way with acceptance and mercy."[141]

St. Bernard of Clairvaux made a similar point: "The sound person feels not the sick one's pains. ... It is fellow sufferers that readily feel compassion for the sick and the hungry. You will never have real mercy for the failings of another until you know and realize that you have the same failings in your soul."[142] Indeed,

216

none of us are fully sound people. We all are fellow sufferers. You might not cheat on your spouse, but you might commit adultery in your heart with lustful glances. You might not murder someone, but you may have killed someone's reputation with your gossip and uncharitable words. You might not have supported abortion, but you have contributed to the culture of death by shunning your responsibility to care for the poor and exhibiting the same individualistic attitude that supports abortion in society. It's in this sense that Bernard says that when you notice someone's faults, you must look inside your own soul and see how "you have the same failings in your soul."

If you lack compassion and tend to judge other people for their faults, it may be an indication that *you* have a deeper moral problem. Perhaps you are looking too much at other people's faults and not enough at your own. And it's not enough to say, "Yes, I'm a sinner. I have a lot of weaknesses." Anyone can say that. But the truly humble person comes to terms with how broken he really is—how weak, proud, and selfish he is, the many ways he hurts others and hurts his relationship with God, how he does not love others as Christ loves him. St. Bernard explains, "If you have eyes for the shortcomings of your neighbor and not for your own, no feeling of mercy will arise in you but rather indignation. You will be more ready to judge than to help, to crush in the spirit of anger than to instruct in the spirit of gentleness."[143]

Put on Compassion

What can we do to root out judging others and cultivate a compassionate heart?

First, never judge someone's heart, their intentions. Always assume the best. St. Catherine says, "Nothing in the world can make it right for you to sit in judgment on the intentions of my servants"[144] and "often ... a person's intention is good; there is no one who can judge the hidden heart."[145] We should always try to bring before our minds the person's good qualities and assume their good intentions and sincere efforts that we don't see. That's what St. Thérèse of Lisieux said she did:

> When ... the devil tries to place before the eyes of my soul the faults of such and such a Sister who is less attractive to me, I hasten to search out her virtues, her good intentions; I tell myself that even if I did see her fall once, she could easily have won a great number of victories which she is hiding through humility, and that even what appears to me as a fault can very easily be an act of virtue because of her intention. ... We must never judge.[146]

Second, always put on compassion. People are more likely to change their ways if they see themselves so gently understood.[147] We can participate in God loving them and healing them. But if they sense our hard, critical, judgmental hearts, they might resist repentance out of pride or give up trying out of discouragement, thinking they can never change, never be understood, or never receive forgiveness.

Third, avoid imposing your latest conversion on others. We often get excited about something new we've learned about living our faith—something about the liturgy, apologetics, a method of prayer, modesty, fasting, or approaches to raising children Catholic—and we quickly expect everyone around us to have the same heightened Catholic sensibilities we just discovered. And we get very frustrated when they don't. "Why don't they see that this is the best form of music for the Liturgy?" "Every good Catholic parent should raise their kids like this." "This form of prayer is the best." But God warned St. Catherine that it is the devil who makes you "want to force all my servants to walk by the same path you yourself follow."[148] What you have come to appreciate may not be something God requires of all faithful Catholics. And even if it does entail a universal moral truth, we still should be patient with others who may not have benefited from the same experiences or formation we did, even as we lead them to the fullness of the truth.

Fourth, we must always be humble. When we notice someone's fault, we might be tempted to think we are somehow a better person, a more faithful Christian, a more virtuous person in that matter. But we should remember that whatever good is happening in our life is not our own. It is all from God. And we should remind ourselves of how it is only by God's grace that we are prevented from making the same mistakes or worse. God instructed St. Catherine to always respond with humility when she noticed someone's faults, saying, "Today it is your turn; tomorrow it will be mine unless divine grace holds me up."

* * * * * *

Is there someone in your life that you tend to relate to more out of judgment in your heart than compassion and mercy? Ask God to give you more compassion for that person, and ask him to help you love that person as he has loved you.

Conclusion:
Continuing the Pilgrimage of Prayer

As we come to the end of our journey, I think again about pilgrimage. Since I've led pilgrimages to Rome and the Holy Land for many years, pilgrims in my groups occasionally ask me, "Do you ever get tired of going back to the same places?"

It's a fair question. The churches don't change. The statues don't change. Even some of the people who work there don't change. Most of the art, windows, and saints in these churches haven't moved for centuries. But even though I revisit the same sacred sites year after year, I sometimes discover something new. I learn some interesting fact, or a pilgrim asks me about a detail in a painting I had never before noticed.

Most often, however, what is new is my *experience* of the place: the same old church touches me in a new way. I am taken in, once again, by the beauty of the basilica, but it moves my heart in a new way today. Perhaps I remember having prayed at a certain spot years ago and thank the Lord for the graces of that pivotal moment. Or maybe the example of the saint buried there inspires me in a certain decision I have to make at present. Or I implore the saint to help me through some new trial I'm facing. It never gets old. There's always something new in my experience of these same sacred places.

The same is true in the spiritual life. The themes in Catholic spirituality discussed in this book—the themes of thirst and trust, surrender and humility, healing and mercy—are not just one-time stops on a spiritual itinerary. We are meant to go back to these over and over again throughout our lives. Like someone ascending a spiral staircase, we go around and around the same themes, the same struggles, the same blessings. But each time we experience them a little differently, from a slightly different angle, maybe just a little bit higher, hopefully with a little more faithfulness, trust, and love. There's always a new grace awaiting us in the twists and turns God takes us on in the interior pilgrimage of prayer.

The night before our pilgrimage groups fly back home, we have a final meal, a "last supper" before departing, and I offer one last challenge to the participants. It's a challenge I'd like to share with you. I encourage the group that before they pack their suitcases, they take just few minutes to do some "spiritual packing": What is the one main thing they want to take away from their pilgrimage and apply to their lives when they return home? Is there one major theme, one aspect of the pilgrimage that touched them most? I ask them to consider how they can commit to live differently when they get back home, in a way that allows them to bring the graces of the pilgrimage into their everyday lives. And then I encourage them to write it down so that they have something to come back to, to help them remember. This will help them allow God to write the pilgrimage on their hearts.

So I will close now by asking you the same question: What is the one theme or insight that touched you the most during your journey through these thirty reflections? What is your most significant takeaway from this journey? In what way do you think God is inviting you to follow him more closely? Think about how you can put this into practice moving forward. Talk to God about it. Ask him about it. Then write it down. Perhaps you can write it down in this book so that you will remember it in the weeks, months, and years to come.

And if you come back to this book down the road, I pray that you will find that the insights you have gained from the saints have changed you—that they were sown deep in your heart and bore fruit in your life. And at that moment, may they be like a beautiful old church that never changes but always changes you. May that wisdom from the Lord encourage you once more in whatever next steps he may be leading you toward in your interior pilgrimage of prayer.

Acknowledgments

Most of this work was written in a beautiful, unique setting: in the presence of the Blessed Sacrament. It was 2020, during the height of the COVID-19 global pandemic. As the world shut down and many churches closed their doors, the parish closest to my home did a wonderful thing. It welcomed the faithful inside its walls to draw near to Jesus, offering Exposition of the Blessed Sacrament in the main sanctuary from seven in the morning to nine at night every day. It is a very large church and so had plenty of room for people to spread out and pray during the crisis. And the parish kept the doors between the sanctuary and the narthex open to maintain good circulation. Those open doors provided me with the chance of a lifetime.

I often bring pen and paper to a chapel to write and edit in front of the Blessed Sacrament. But I don't usually type on my laptop in the sacred space so as not to disturb others. However, with the Eucharist exposed in the main sanctuary of this parish and the sanctuary doors wide open, I was able to sit and kneel outside in the narthex and write much of this book in the presence of our Lord without distracting anyone in prayer. I would kneel in the narthex, read a passage from a saint, look up at our Lord in the Eucharist, pray, write a few lines, and then pray some more. It was a tremendous gift to spend many hours from March to May 2020 praying and writing in this way. So my first word of thanks goes to St. Thomas More Parish in Centennial, Colorado, for welcoming the faithful to pray during this difficult time and for giving me the unique opportunity to write a book on prayer and the interior life in such a prayerful way, close to our Lord in the Blessed Sacrament.

I also acknowledge the many teachers, spiritual directors, and friends who have had an impact on my own interior life, including Bishop Carl Mengling, Fr. John Hardon, SJ, and Sister Susan Piper. The most thanks goes to Fr. Paul Murray, OP, teacher, mentor, and friend. His classes on spiritual theology at the Angelicum in Rome and our many conversations over the last thirty years have shaped my teaching and writing on this topic and, even more, have affected my own spiritual life in profound ways. Though I quote Fr. Murray often in this book, no doubt the influence of his wisdom touches almost every page as much as it has touched my soul. Whatever insights the reader may gain from this work come from the saints and many teachers and writers who have taught me so much, most especially Fr. Murray.

I also thank the many FOCUS missionaries whom I have taught on these themes throughout the years. In particular, I am grateful for those missionaries who read sections of this book and gave me valuable feedback, including Erin Falbo, Jessica Navin, Stephanie Parks, Fallon Scanlan, and Carrie Wagner. Particular thanks goes to Kyrstn Bishop, who reviewed the original manuscript and developed most of the reflection questions. Finally, I thank my wife, Beth, not only for her insights on the manuscript but for our many ongoing conversations over the years on spiritual theology and the interior life.

Appendix:
How to Pray

If you are reading this appendix, chances are you already have some desire to pray—to learn about prayer, pray more consistently, or grow deeper in prayer. Or perhaps you are somewhat new to prayer and are unsure how to get started. Wherever you are in your journey with God and prayer, know that God has brought you here to this point, and he will help you take the next step with him in prayer. For the desire to pray itself is the beginning of prayer. God put that desire on your heart. He will continue to draw you closer to him in prayer. All you need to do is respond.

The following guide offers a few basic practical tips on how to pray. Whether you are just beginning in prayer or looking for a refresher to deepen your prayer life, I hope these points will be helpful for you to go deeper with the Lord in prayer.

Preparation: Time, Place, Inner Quiet

To begin prayer well, we should prepare our hearts and minds for our time with God. Just as we desire to give our full attention to those we love when we are with them, so we want to be fully present to God when we spend time with him in prayer.

First, we should *set a time* for prayer each day. As Pope Francis says, the soul needs prayer as the body needs oxygen. That's why we need to take in "the deep breath of prayer"[149] each day. But prayer often will not happen if we don't make it a priority and schedule it. We are busy. If we don't plan a time each day for prayer, other things will take up our time and we will forget our time with God.

Second, we need to *find a quiet place* to pray: a church, a Eucharistic Adoration chapel, a quiet place at home, a peaceful place outdoors. The key is to find a peaceful setting that has fewer chances for interruptions and distractions so you can give your full attention to God.

Third, we need to *quiet ourselves interiorly*. Close our doors. Close our screens. Turn off our phones and devices, or at least put them on silent mode. Put away our to-do lists. Stop humming that song that's stuck in our head. We cannot give God our hearts fully in prayer if we have incessant buzzes, beeps, notifications, and updates constantly vying for our attention. Nor can we be present to God if we're constantly worrying about problems at work, projects to get done, and the schedule for the day. God is longing for us just to spend some time with him. We need to create a quiet space in our hearts to meet him.

How to Start: Sign of the Cross and Recalling God's Presence

Start your time in prayer by making the Sign of the Cross. This ancient prayer calls on God's name: Father, Son, and Holy Spirit. In Scripture, to call on the Lord's name is to invoke his presence. So when we make the Sign of the Cross, we are inviting God to be with us when we pray.

Next, take a few moments—perhaps a few minutes or even just a few seconds—to quiet yourself and *be aware of the presence of God with you*, as he himself said, "Be still, and know that I am God" (Psalm 46:10). Set aside your worries, your many pressing tasks and responsibilities, and recognize that God is present to you. He's always there, but now you are taking time to be aware of his presence as you approach him in prayer. He loves you. He is longing for your heart and your attention. He longs for you to talk to him as a friend. And he yearns for you to listen to him in the stillness of your soul.

Conversation with God: A-C-T-S

There are several methods of prayer, but for beginners, here are four simple ways to start having a conversation with God. They can be summed up with the letters A-C-T-S, which stand for adoration, confession, thanksgiving, and supplication.

Adoration

When we approach God in prayer, we first should acknowledge that we are not talking with any ordinary person. We are entering into conversation with the Almighty, All-Holy God himself! Adoration is the fundamental humble attitude we should have when we begin prayer—showing homage before God, approaching him with profound respect and reverence, recognizing that he is God.

How do we do this? We can adore God in our *words* by telling him we love him: "I love you, O LORD, my strength!" (Psalm 18:1).

One of the best ways we express our adoration of God is through *praise*. This is simply lauding God for who he is as God, not just for what he does for us. "Praise the LORD! Praise God in his sanctuary; praise him in his mighty firmament! Praise him for his mighty deeds; praise him according to his exceeding greatness!" (Psalm 150:1–2).

We might also express adoration through a respectful *silence*, being in awe of who he is or of being in his holy presence.

Even our *posture* in prayer can express that we adore God. Whether we're kneeling, sitting, or standing, we should do so not in a sloppy, casual way during prayer but in a respectful way, realizing we are in the presence of the King of Kings and Lord of Lords.

Confession

Second, we can *confess our sins to God* and tell him we are sorry. This is another essential part of any close relationship. When we hurt someone we love, we should acknowledge it and express our sorrow over what we have done.

We can do the same in prayer. We can take a moment simply acknowledge our sinfulness and tell the Lord we are sorry. "Lord, I am sorry for my sins. Please forgive me." As the psalmist cries out, "Have mercy on me, O God. ... Wash me thoroughly from my iniquity, and cleanse me from my sin!" (Psalm 51:1–2).

Thanksgiving

Third, *we thank the Lord* for his many blessings. We can thank him for a beautiful sunset, for peace, for our life. We can thank him for our health, for our family, for our work, for the ways he has helped us. We can thank him for his forgiveness, for his Real Presence in the Eucharist, for the gift of salvation he has offered us on the Cross. Most of all, we can thank God for who he is, for his love, for his mercy, for his grace in our lives.

Acknowledging the goodness and kindness of others is important for any close relationship. It's especially important to do with God. "O give thanks to the LORD, for he is good, for his mercy endures for ever" (Psalm 136:1).

Supplication

Supplication is a Biblical word for a request one brings to God. God wants us to *bring our needs to him* humbly and earnestly: "Have no anxiety about anything, but in everything by prayer and supplication with thanksgiving let your requests be made known to God" (Philippians 4:6). We can bring our supplications to the Lord in two ways.

First, we should pray for other people and their needs before our own. This is called *intercession*. We can pray for our family, friends, coworkers, and benefactors. We can intercede for the poor and the suffering. We can pray for someone's healing from illness. We also can pray for conversions, interceding for those who are living a life far removed from the Gospel and for those who do not believe in Christ.

Second, we bring our own needs to the Lord. This is sometimes referred to as the prayer of *petition*. We ask the Lord to bless our work, to bless our family, to solve a problem, and to alleviate a suffering we are experiencing. We also ask him to help us spiritually—to overcome sin, to trust him more, to show us his will, to give us the grace to follow him more closely, to surrender to his plan for our lives and not cling to our own.

When we make prayers of supplication, we express our needs, but we trust that that God's plan is always better than what whatever we might imagine. So we express our supplications humbly, confident that God always answers our prayers, but not always in the way we want or in the time we want. As we say in the Lord's Prayer, *thy will be done.*

In summary, we should remember ACTS. We can use these four basic ways of talking with God as part of our regular time in prayer:

Adoration: Tell God you love him. Praise him. Adore him.

Confession: Acknowledge your sins, and tell God you are sorry for them.

Thanksgiving: Thank the Lord for who he is and for his many blessings in your life.

Supplication: Bring your requests to the Lord, interceding for other people and presenting petitions for your own life.

Meditation

ACTS is a basic, introductory way to begin having a conversation with God in prayer. It is a kind of vocal prayer, in which we use words—either audible words or words we say in our hearts. But there is another method of prayer, known as "meditation" or "mental prayer," that the Church encourages us to use regularly.

Don't think of meditation as something complex or esoteric. It's a simple form of prayer many ordinary Christians have used throughout the ages. It involves the mind seeking to understand Jesus, his life, and his message better. It usually involves reflecting on a Scriptural passage or a spiritual text such as a saint's writings or a reflection from a spiritual writer. We read a line or two from the Bible or a book. Then we pause, reflect on it, ponder how it applies to our lives, and talk to God about it. "Lord, how does this speak to me now? What might you be inviting me to consider in this passage for my life?" Meditation engages our thoughts, imagination, emotions, and desires.

Ignatian Meditation

One popular expression of this kind of prayer is known as *Ignatian meditation*, named after the sixteenth-century Spanish founder of the Jesuits, St. Ignatius of Loyola. Ignatius encouraged Christians to put themselves in the Biblical scenes and imagine being present as the events unfolded. So while meditating on the Gospel story of the wedding feast at Cana, for example, we imagine the smell of the good food, the taste of the good wine, and the sounds of joy, music, and laughter. We prayerfully imagine the sudden shock the leaders of the feast had when they noticed they had run out of wine. We picture Mary rushing to tell Jesus, "They have no wine" (John 2:3). Then we see Jesus turning to the servants and saying, "Fill the jars with wine" (John 2:7). Perhaps we even put ourselves in the shoes of those servants at that moment, wondering, "What good will *this* do? A bunch of jars with water? How does that solve the problem of the wine shortage?" From a human perspective, Jesus' command does not seem helpful. But if we were those servants, would we trust Jesus even though his command doesn't make sense to us?

Ignatius encourages us to engage our senses, imagine being in the biblical scene, and so in prayer encounter Christ today as those servants did at Cana some two thousand years ago. This is one form of meditative prayer.

Lectio Divina

Another classical way of praying with Scripture is called *lectio divina*, which means "divine reading." This method goes back to the early Church and immerses a person in the Scriptures by reading a passage multiple times, reflecting prayerfully on God's inspired words, and paying attention to the way the Holy Spirit may be speaking to you through this passage.

Lectio divina has four stages:

- *Lectio* (read). First, select a short section of Scripture. It can be anything from the Bible or perhaps a reading from Mass that day. Then read the passage slowly in order to become familiar with it. As you do so, listen carefully and see if a certain word or phrase happens to jump out and grab your attention.

- *Meditatio* (meditate and reflect). Read the passage a second time, but when you do so, pause and linger on the word or phrase that stands out to you. Ponder that word, considering its meaning and reflecting on why it caught your attention.

- *Oratio* (respond in prayer). Read the passage yet again. But this time, talk to God about it. Respond to his Word with love. Tell the Lord what moved you about the passage. Ask the Lord what he might be trying to show you through this passage, phrase, or word. Ask him how his Word might apply to your life right now or how he might be inviting you to draw closer to him through the message of this passage. This is the time for dialogue, for an intimate conversation with God.

- *Contemplatio* (contemplate—rest in God's presence). Simply sit quietly in the presence of God and rest in whatever graces, insights, or challenges you may have received during your time with God's Word in prayer. Express your love for God and your gratitude to him for those blessings and resolve to draw closer to him.

Prayer Is About the Heart

Whatever expression or method of prayer you use, don't stress about it. Prayer is not primarily about which technique one uses and how well the soul carries it out. Prayer is not primarily about one's performance. It's about the heart. The key is just to get started. Simply telling God that you *want* to pray—or even humbly admitting you're not sure what to do in prayer and asking God for him to help you—is itself a beautiful gift you can give to God. He rejoices when you come to him humbly, as you are, and we can trust that his grace will be there to help you when you pray.

Notes

1   Benedict XVI, General Audience (January 31, 2007), vatican.va.

2   Mother Teresa said that these words point to the very heart of the purpose of the Missionaries of Charity: "We have these words in every chapel of the MCs to remind us what an MC is here for: to quench the thirst of Jesus for souls, for love, for kindness, for compassion, for delicate love." Mother Teresa, *Where There is Love, There is God*, ed. Brian Kolodiejchuk (New York: Image, 2010), 51. Ever since her call to serve the poorest of the poor in 1946, Mother Teresa insisted that the Missionaries of Charity were founded "to satiate the thirst of Jesus," and she included this statement in the founding rules for the new religious order: "The General End of the Missionaries of Charity is to satiate the thirst of Jesus Christ on the Cross for Love and Souls" (40–41).

3   Teresa of Calcutta, Letter to the Missionary of Charity Sisters (April 24, 1996), quoted in Joseph Langford, *Mother Teresa's Secret Fire* (Huntington, IN: Our Sunday Visitor, 2008), 51.

4   Paul Murray, *I Loved Jesus in the Night: Teresa of Calcutta—A Secret Revealed* (Brewster, MA: Paraclete, 2008), 73.

5   Langford, *Secret Fire*, 281–282.

6   Mother Teresa, *Where There Is Love*, 52.

7   Mother Teresa, Varanasi letter (March 25, 1993), in Langford, *Secret Fire*, 55.

8   Catherine of Siena to her niece, Sister Eugenia, Letter 26, in *Catherine of Siena: Passion for the Truth, Compassion for Humanity*, ed. Mary O'Driscoll (New York: New City Press, 2005), 22, archive.org.

9   Catherine to Sister Eugenia, 22.

10   Francis, *Evangelii Gaudium* (November 24, 2013), 262, vatican.va.

11   Jacques Philippe, *Time for God: A Guide to Mental Prayer,* trans. Helena Scott (New York: Scepter Publishers, 1992), 27–28.

12   Philippe, 19.

13   Edward Sri, *Love Unveiled: The Catholic Faith Explained* (San Francisco: Ignatius Press, 2015), 270.

14   Langford, *Secret Fire*, 162. Mother Teresa adapted the prayer from "Jesus, the Light of the Soul," by John Henry Newman, *Everyday Meditations* (Manchester, NH: Sophia Institute Press, 2013), 85–87.

15   John of the Cross, "Spiritual Canticle" 29.3, quoted in Philippe, *Time for God*, 31–32.

16   John Henry Newman, quoted in Langford, *Secret Fire*, 162.

17   Murray, *I Loved Jesus in the Night*, 72.

18   Thomas Aquinas, *Summa Theologica* II-II.83.13.

19   Simon Tugwell, *Ways of Imperfection: An Exploration of Christian Spirituality* (Springfield: Templegate, 1985), 139.

20   Catherine to Sister Eugenia, 22–23. See also Catherine of Siena, *The Dialogue*, trans. Suzanne Noffke (New York: Paulist, 1980), 101.

21   Catherine, *Dialogue* 107, in Noffke, 201.

22   Catherine 60, in Noffke, 113.

23   See Catherine 60.

24   Catherine 60.

25   Catherine 60.

26   Catherine 60.

27   Catherine 78, in Noffke, 147.

28   Catherine 107, in Noffke, 201.

29   Maria Faustina Kowalska, *Diary: Divine Mercy in My Soul* (Stockbridge, MA: Marian Press, 1985), 41.

30   William Johnston, ed., *The Cloud of Unknowing and the Book of Privy Counseling* (New York: Doubleday, 1973), 49.

31   C. S. Lewis, *Mere Christianity* (New York: Harper Collins, 2001), 136–137.

32   Simon Tugwell, *Prayer: Living with God* (Springfield, IL: Templegate, 1975), vii.

33   Philippe, *Time for God*, 24.

34   Mother Teresa, *Come Be My Light: The Private Writings of the Saint of Calcutta,* ed. Brian Kolodiejchuk (New York: Image, 2007), 47.

35   Mother Teresa, 28.

36   Mother Teresa, 48.

37   Mother Teresa, 48–49.

38   Mother Teresa, 49.

39   Mother Teresa, 49.

40   Ignatius of Loyola, *Spiritual Exercises* (TAN Books, 1999), 167.

41   John Paul II, Homily for the Inauguration of His Pontificate (October 22, 1978), 5, vatican.va.

42   Karol Wojtyla (John Paul II), *Love and Responsibility*, trans. H. T. Willetts (San Francisco: Ignatius Press, 1993), 126.

43   Mother Teresa, *Come Be My Light*, 24.

44   Benedict XVI, Homily (April 24, 2005), vatican.va.

45   Thérèse of Lisieux, quoted in Jacques Philippe, *Searching for and Maintaining Peace* (Staten Island: Society of St. Paul, 2002), 38.

46   Catherine, *Dialogue* 140, in Noffke, 287.

47   Wilfrid Stinissen, *Into Your Hands, Father: Abandoning Ourselves to the God Who Loves Us* (San Francisco: Ignatius, 2011), 80.

48   Catherine, *Dialogue* 119, in O'Driscoll, 96–97.

49   Catherine to her brother Benincasa, Letter 18, in O'Driscoll, 21.

50   Etty Hillesum, *An Interrupted Life: The Diaries, 1941–1943* (New York: Henry Holt, 1996), 218.

51   Mother Mary Francis, *A Time for Renewal* (San Francisco: Ignatius, 2015), 83–84.

52   Catherine, *Dialogue* 145, in O'Driscoll, 101.

53   Catherine 145, in O'Driscoll, 101.

54   Catherine 43, in Noffke, 88.

55   Bernard of Clairvaux, *On the Song of Songs* 36.5.

56   Catherine, *Dialogue* 153, in O'Driscoll, 89–90.

57   Catherine 13, in O'Driscoll, 99.

58   Bernard, *On the Song of Songs* 36.6.

59   John Paul II, Homily for the Seventeenth World Youth Day (July 28, 2002), 5, vatican.va.

60   John Paul II, *Dives et Misericordia* (November 30, 1980), 6, vatican.va.

61   Thérèse of Lisieux, "Counsels and Reminiscences," in *The Story of the Soul*, trans. Thomas N. Taylor (New York: Cosimo, 2007), 194–195.

62   Jacques Philippe, *Searching for and Maintaining Peace*, 58–59.

63   "He told me that my failings did not displease the good God. I hold his place at this moment in your regard. Well then, I assure you that he is well satisfied with your soul." August Piere Laveille, *The Life of St. Thérèse of Lisieux*, trans. M. Fitzsimons (Notre Dame, IN: Christian Classics, 2017), 185–186. St. Thérèse took this insight to refer not to serious intentional sin but to our defects, "the little offenses" that are committed against God or others "involuntarily." See Thérèse, *Story of a Soul: The Autobiography of St. Therese of Lisieux*, 3rd ed., trans. John Clarke (Washington, DC: ICS Publications, 1996), 174.

64   Thérèse, *Story of a Soul*, 207.

65   Thérèse, 207.

66   Thérèse, 207.

67   Thérèse, xii.

68   Thérèse, xii.

69   Thérèse, 208.

70   "We must do everything in our power, give without counting the cost, practice virtue at every opportunity, deny ourselves constantly, prove our love by all kinds of attentions and marks of affection, in a word, do all the good deeds in our power for the love of God. But since all that is really very little, it is important to place all our trust in him who alone sanctifies all deeds and can sanctify without them. ... That is what 'the little way of childhood' is all about." Christopher O'Mahoney, *St. Therese of Lisieux by Those Who Knew Her: Testimonies from the Process of Beatification* (Veritas Publications, 1975), 137.

71   Thérèse to Sister Geneviève [Celine], Letter 243 (June 7, 1897), in *Saint Thérèse of Lisieux: General Correspondence*, vol. 2, *1890–1897*, trans. John Clarke (Washington, DC: ICS Publications, 1988), 1122, original emphasis.

72   Faustina, *Diary*, 723.

73   Sister Marie of the Sacred Heart to Thérèse, Letter 196 (September 13, 1896), in *General Correspondence* 2, 997.

74   Thérèse to Sister Marie of the Sacred Heart, Letter 197 (September 17, 1896), in *General Correspondence* 2, 999, original emphasis.

75   Bernard of Clairvaux, *On the Song of Songs* 56.

76   Thérèse, *Story of a Soul*, xi, emphasis added.

77   Thérèse to Marie Guerin, Letter 92 (May 30, 1889), in *General Correspondence*, vol. 1 (1982), 568.

78   Mother Mary Francis, *Time of Renewal*, 24.

79   Faustina Maria Pia, "The Litany of Trust," Sisters of Life (sistersoflife.org). Used by permission. Please visit the website to obtain individual copies of the litany.

80   "Healing is an essential dimension of the apostolic mission and of faith in general. ... When understood at sufficiently deep level, this expresses the entire content of 'redemption.'" Joseph Ratzinger (Pope Benedict XVI), *Jesus of Nazareth: From the Baptism in the Jordan to the Transfiguration* (New York: Doubleday, 2007), 176.

81   Aquinas, *Summa Theologica* II-II.155.4.

82   Tugwell, *Prayer*, 104–105.

83   My brief summary of these four stages is based on the excellent treatment of Thomistic ethics in Steven Jensen, *Living the Good Life* (Washington: CUA Press, 2014), 60–96, and William Mattison, *Introducing Moral Theology* (Grand Rapids: Brazos, 2008), 75–94.

84   Aquinas, *Summa Theologica* I-II.24.3.

85   Mattison, *Introducing Moral Theology*, 86.

86   Augustine of Hippo, *A Treatise on the Spirit and the Letter*, trans. Peter Holmes and Robert Earnest Wallis (Savage, MN: Lighthouse, 2018), chapter 34.

87   Teresa of Calcutta, Varanasi letter, in Langford, *Secret Fire*, 55.

88   Benedict XVI, *Spe Salvi* (November 30, 2007), 39, vatican.va.

89   Wilfrid Stinissen, *Into Your Hands Father*, 40.

90   Jacques Philippe, *Interior Freedom*, trans. Helena Scott (New York: Scepter, 2007), 58.

91   John of the Cross, *Spiritual Canticle*, stanza 32, in *Impact of God: Soundings of St. John of the Cross*, trans. Iain Matthew (London: Hodder and Stoughton, 1995), 29.

92   For a fuller treatment, see Donald Haggerty, *St. John of the Cross: Master of Contemplation* (San Francisco: Ignatius Press, 2022), and Matthew, *Impact of God*.

93   John of the Cross, *The Living Flame of Love* 3.18, in *The Collected Works of St. John of the Cross,* trans. Kieran Kavanaugh and Otilio Rodriguez (Washington, DC: ICS Publications, 1991), 617.

94   Augustine, *Confessions* 1.1.

95   John of the Cross, *The Ascent of Mount Carmel* 1.13.6, trans. Edward Sri.

96   John of the Cross 1.13.11, trans. Edward Sri.

97   John of the Cross 1.13.4, in *Collected Works.*

98   John of the Cross, *Sayings of Light and Love* 15, in Matthew, 44.

99   John of the Cross, *Ascent,* 1.11.4, in *Collected Works.*

100   John of the Cross 2.7.8.

101   Teresa of Avila to King Philip, Letter 211 (April 12, 1577).

102   Testimony of Alonso de la Madre de Dios, *Biblioteca Mistica Carmelitana* 14.387.

103   Gerald Brennan, *St. John of the Cross: His Life and Poetry* (London: Cambridge University Press, 1973). The third line is translated by Edward Sri.

104   John of the Cross, *Spiritual Canticle,* stanza 1, in Matthew, 10.

105   John of the Cross, *The Dark Night* 1.3.3, in *Collected Works.*

106   John of the Cross 1.1.1–3.

107   John of the Cross 1.7.5.

108   John of the Cross 1.8.3.

109   John of the Cross 1.10.2.

110   John of the Cross 1.10.4.

111   John of the Cross 1.10.4–5.

112   John of the Cross 1.10.6.

113   John of the Cross , *Ascent* 1.1, in *Collected Works.*

114   Gregory I, *Book Two of the Dialogues: Life of St. Benedict,* prologue, osb.org.

115   Søren Kierkegaard, quoted in Peter Kreeft, *Making Choices* (Ann Arbor: Servant Books, 1990), n140, archive.org.

116   Mother Teresa, *A Gift for God* (London: Collins, 1975), 82–83.

117   Bernard of Clairvaux, *De Consideratione* II, in Jean-Baptiste Chautard, *The Soul of the Apostolate* (Trappist, KY: Abbey of Gethsemani, 1946), 74–75.

118   John Henry Newman, "The World Our Enemy," sermon 3, in *Parochial and Plain Sermons*, vol. 7 (London: Longmans, Green, 1891), 30.

119   Newman, 34.

120   Newman, 34.

121   Raymond of Capua, *Life* 2.1.121, in O'Driscoll, 9.

122   Catherine, *Dialogue* 64, in Noffke, 121. The key is the difference between loving out of duty and loving freely. God loves freely. But we can't love God back freely—we owe him all our love out of duty. "I ask you to love me with the same love with which I love you. But for me you cannot do this, for I loved you without being loved. Whatever love you have for me you owe me, so you love me not gratuitously but out of duty, while I love you not out of duty but gratuitously. So you cannot give me the kind of love I ask of you" (64). This is why God puts us among our neighbors: so that we can do for them what we cannot do for God. We can love our neighbor not merely out of duty, but freely, expecting nothing back. "And whatever you do for them I will consider done for me" (64; see Matthew 25:40).

123   Catherine, *Dialogue* 7, in Noffke, 37.

124   Catherine to Caterina di Scetto, Letter 50, in O'Driscoll, 27.

125   Thérèse, *Story of a Soul,* 221.

126   Thérèse, 221.

127   Christopher O'Mahoney, *Testimonies,* 132.

128   Thérèse, *Story of a Soul,* 246.

129   Thérèse, 222, original emphasis.

130   Thérèse, 222.

131   Marie of the Sacred Heart (witness 3), Statement in Canonization Process for Thérèse, Session 25, September 12, 1910, Carmel of Lisieux archives, archives-carmel-lisieux.fr/.

132   Thérèse, *Story of a Soul,* 223.

133   Thérèse, 220.

134   Francis of Assisi, *The Testament* 3, in *Francis of Assisi: Early Documents,* vol. 1, ed. Regis J. Armstrong, J. A. Wayne Hellmann, and William J. Short (New York: New City Press, 1999), 124.

135   Francis of Assisi, 124.

136 Catherine, *Dialogue* 102, in Noffke, 193.

137 Catherine 108, in Noffke, 202.

138 O'Mahoney, *Testimonies*, 132.

139 O'Mahoney, 50–51.

140 O'Mahoney, 94.

141 Francis of Assisi, *The Name of God Is Mercy* (New York: Random House, 2016), 67.

142 Bernard of Clairvaux, *The Steps of Humility and Pride* 6, in M. Basil Pennington, ed., *Bernard of Clairvaux: A Lover Teaching the Way of Love* (Hyde Park, NY: New City Press, 1997), 63.

143 Bernard, 63.

144 Catherine, *Dialogue* 105, in Noffke, 197.

145 Catherine 100, in Noffke, 191.

146 Thérèse, *Story of a Soul*, 221.

147 Catherine, *Dialogue* 102, in Noffke, 194.

148 Catherine 104, in Noffke, 196.

149 Francis, *Evangelii Gaudium* (November 24, 2013), 262, vatican.va.

About the Author

Dr. Edward Sri is a theologian, author, and well-known Catholic speaker who appears regularly on EWTN. Each year he speaks to tens of thousands of people from around the world, including clergy, parish leaders, catechists, and laity.

He has written several best-selling books, including *No Greater Love: A Biblical Walk Through Christ's Passion, Walking with Mary,* and *Who Am I to Judge? Responding to Relativism with Logic and Love.*

He is also the presenter of several faith formation film series, including *A Biblical Walk Through the Mass, Mary: A Biblical Walk with the Blessed Mother,* and *Follow Me: Meeting Jesus in the Gospel of John* and is the host of the film series *Symbolon: The Catholic Faith Explained.*

Dr. Sri is a founding leader of FOCUS, the Fellowship of Catholic University Students, where he currently serves as senior vice president of apostolic outreach. He leads pilgrimages to Rome and the Holy Land each year and is the host of the weekly podcast *All Things Catholic.* He holds a doctorate from the Pontifical University of St. Thomas Aquinas in Rome and is an adjunct professor at the Augustine Institute. He lives with his wife, Elizabeth, and their eight children in Littleton, Colorado.

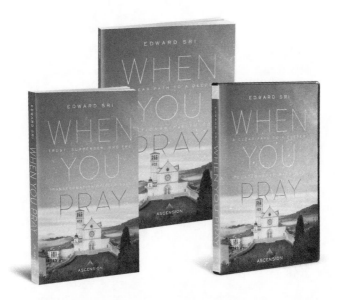